GLADSTONE

GREAT LIVES

1.	SHAKESPEARE	*by* JOHN DRINKWATER
2.	QUEEN VICTORIA	ARTHUR PONSONBY (LORD PONSONBY)
3.	WAGNER	W. J. TURNER
4.	JOHN WESLEY	BONAMY DOBRÉE
5.	JOSHUA REYNOLDS	JOHN STEEGMANN
6.	CECIL RHODES	J. G. LOCKHART
7.	GLADSTONE	FRANCIS BIRRELL
8.	GEORGE ELIOT	ANNE FREMANTLE
9.	THE BRONTËS	IRENE COOPER WILLIS
10.	CHARLES II	JOHN HAYWARD
11.	DICKENS	BERNARD DARWIN
12.	BEETHOVEN	ALAN PRYCE-JONES
13.	H. M. STANLEY	A. J. A. SYMONS
14.	WILLIAM BLAKE	ALAN CLUTTON-BROCK
15.	SHERIDAN	W. A. DARLINGTON
16.	ROBERT BURNS	CATHERINE CARSWELL
17.	EDWARD VII	H. E. WORTHAM
18.	THACKERAY	G. U. ELLIS

To be published shortly

NELSON	*by* BRIAN TUNSTALL
THE PRINCE CONSORT	HAMISH MILES
POPE	JOHN SPARROW
MILTON	ROSE MACAULAY
COBDEN	I. I. BOWEN
HAIG	BRIG.-GEN. J. CHARTERIS
NAPOLEON III	GRAHAM BROOKS
BYRON	PETER QUENNELL
VAN GOGH	PETER BURRA

Other volumes in preparation

GLADSTONE

by FRANCIS BIRRELL

Great Lives

DUCKWORTH
3 HENRIETTA STREET
LONDON W.C.2

First published March 1933
Second Impression June 1933

To
DAVID GOURLAY

Made *and* printed *in* Great Britain
By The Camelot Press Ltd
London *and* Southampton

CONTENTS

CHRONOLOGY

1809.	Dec. 9th.	Born.
1832.	Dec. 13th.	Elected for Newark.
1837.	Jan. 27th.	Under-Secretary for the Colonies.
1841.	Sept. 3rd.	Vice-President of the Board of Trade.
1843.	May 15th.	President of the Board of Trade.
1845.	Jan. 28th.	Retires from the Cabinet on the Maynooth Grant.
1845.	Dec. 23rd.	Appointed Colonial Secretary.
1847.	Aug. 3rd.	Elected for Oxford University.
1852.	Dec. 23rd.	Chancellor of the Exchequer.
1855.	Jan. 30th.	Resignation of the Aberdeen Ministry.
1855.	Feb. 22nd.	Resigns from the Palmerston Ministry.
1859.	Jan. 20th.	Chancellor of the Exchequer in the Palmerston Administration.
1860.	Feb. 10th.	Introduces Budget, incorporating the Commercial Treaty with France.
1865.	July 18th.	Defeated for Oxford University.
1865.	July 22nd.	Elected for South Lancashire.

1868.	Nov. 17th.	Elected for Greenwich.
1868.	Nov. 24th.	Defeated for South-West Lancashire.
1868.	Dec. 9th.	Forms First Administration.
1874.	Feb. 4th.	Re-elected for Greenwich.
1874.	Feb. 17th.	Resigns from the leadership.
1877.	May 7th.	Moves first of his resolutions on the Eastern question.
1879.	Nov. 25th.	Opens the Midlothian Campaign.
1880.	April 5th.	Elected for Midlothian.
1880.	April 28th.	Forms the Second Administration.
1885.	June 9th.	Resignation of the Second Administration.
1886.	Feb. 3rd.	Forms the Third Administration.
1886.	April 8th.	Introduces First Home Rule Bill.
1886.	July 20th.	Resignation of the Third Administration.
1892.	Aug. 15th.	Forms the Fourth Administration.
1893.	Feb. 3rd.	Introduces Second Home Rule Bill.
1894.	Mar. 1st.	On the Lords' Amendments to the Parish Councils Bill.
1894.	Mar. 3rd.	Resigns the Premiership.
1898.	May 19th.	Death of Mr. Gladstone.

CHAPTER I

Birth – Eton – Oxford – entry into Parliament – Board of Trade – resignation over Maynooth – Colonial Office – repeal of the Corn Laws – split in the Tory Party – resignation of Sir Robert Peel.

In September 1887 Cardinal Manning noted in his diary, with some complacency but not without a measure of truth, " I forsook all things for faith ; he [Gladstone] has forsaken his whole political past for Ireland. He is as isolated now as I was then. And this makes me turn to him. We are at last and at least agreed in this." It is the duty of the biographer to explain how it came to be that the well-to-do son of a Jamaica slave-owner, the Coningsby Etonian, the Christ Church double first, who had been returned to the first reformed Parliament for a pocket borough to preach the theocracy of the Established Church, came to find himself, at the age of seventy-eight, in the painful position described by Cardinal Manning. Not that the problem presented any great difficulty to Manning. " His course has been to me intelligible from the first. He began as a Tory. I was, as I said, a Mosaic Radical. His Toryism was only a boyish and Etonian admiration for Canning, and an intimacy with [Lord] Lincoln and the like."

But as what was clear to Manning may not be so self-evident to everybody else, we will look into the matter more closely.

In 1890, when the Liverpool slave-owner's boy had been for ten years the Radical member for Midlothian, he boasted at Dundee, as is the way with English representatives of Scotch constituencies, that he " had not a drop of English blood in his veins." For once the boast was justified. William Ewart Gladstone was born on December 29th, 1809, at 62 Rodney Street, Liverpool. But his family were recent arrivals in that famous town. " Thomas Gladstones, grandfather of him with whom we are concerned, made his way from Biggar to Leith and there set up in a modest way as corndealer, wholesale and retail. His wife was a Neilson of Springfield. To them sixteen children were born, and John Gladstones[1] (b. December 11th, 1764) was their eldest son. Having established himself in Liverpool, he married in 1792 Jane Hall, a lady of that city, who died without children, six years later. In 1800 he took for his second wife Anne Robertson of Dingwall. Her father was of the clan Donnachaidh, and her mother was of kin with Mackenzies, Munros, and other highland stocks. Their son was therefore of unmixed Scottish origins, half highland, half lowland borderer." Perhaps we may find in this origin some clue to the extraordinary mixture of excitability and canniness, so characteristic of the statesman, which was to mystify all and exasperate many.

[1] He dropped the " s " in 1787 thinking the plural ending of his name sounded awkwardly in the style of the firm Corrie, Gladstones & Grant.

The firm of Corrie, Gladstone & Grant prospered, and Gladstone was always well off. It was an East India house. But unfortunately John Gladstone became "the owner of extensive plantations of sugar and coffee in the West Indies," that is to say, he was a slave-owner and frequently in hot water about his slaves. William defended his father in what was almost his maiden speech. But, whatever may have been old Mr. Gladstone's business necessities, his moral principles were above reproach. A fervent slave-owner, he was an equally fervent Evangelical. He was also a keen politician of the Liberal-Tory school, and in 1812 brought Canning to contest Liverpool against Brougham. It took his son the best part of half a century to get over a fortuitous acquaintance made when he was three years old.[1] Loyalty, amounting to spiritual dependence, was ever one of his leading characteristics.

Gladstone was always busy on his autobiography, analysing his motives and scraping his conscience. Of his childhood he writes at an unknown date: "My religious recollections are a sad blank. Neither was I a popular boy, though not egregiously otherwise. If I was not a bad boy, I think I was a boy with a great absence of goodness. I was a child of slow, in some points, I think, of singularly slow, development. There was more in me perhaps than in the average boy,

[1] "I was set upon one of the chairs standing and directed to say to the company, 'Ladies and Gentlemen.'"

but it required greatly more time to set itself in order and just so in adult and in middle and later life, I acquired very tardily any knowledge of the world, and that simultaneous conspectus of the relations of persons and things, which is necessary for the proper performance of duties in the world." This unflattering self-portrait sounds convincing and we are not helped by it to understand why much more trouble was taken with his than with his brothers' education. He went to Eton in September 1821 and remained there till Christmas 1827. Though for him Eton characteristically remained the "Queen of Schools,"[1] his prolonged residence calls for little comment, save that Arthur Hallam excited in him the romantic admiration that he aroused subsequently in Tennyson. In 1893, convinced that everybody else must be as interested in Hallam as he still was, he wrote to the Queen on the death of Tennyson:

"He [Mr. Gladstone] supposes himself to be the only person still living possessed of early recollections of Tennyson, who called upon him about 1837 and impressed him very deeply. The honour of that visit was due not to any merit or distinction of Mr. Gladstone's, but to a common friendship with Arthur Hallam, whom Tennyson had so profoundly known and loved at Cambridge and who had previously been Mr. Gladstone's closest associate at Eton. Mr. Gladstone is

[1] It is creditable to the "Queen of Schools" that we may see in Upper School busts not only of Gray and Porson, but of Mr. Fox and Mr. Gladstone.

happy in possessing a number of Arthur Hallam's letters: it occurs to him that on account of Your Majesty's feelings towards Tennyson the perusal of these letters might be of interest to Your Majesty. Should this be so, he would do himself the honour to forward them: otherwise he begs Your Majesty not to take the trouble of noticing the proposal, the thought of the moment." The Queen apparently did not "notice the proposal." Still, it is good to know that Hallam's letters to Gladstone have not gone the way of his letters to Tennyson.

"When I was at Eton," said Gladstone, "we knew very little indeed, but we knew it accurately." He studied the classics and learned French, and French remained, despite Dante and Leopardi, among his favourite languages to the end. At the age of eighty he was to embark on Zola. And his affection for French literature extended to the French as a nation. He developed a gift for oratory, and deplored to "Pop" the execution of Charles I. He was a virtuous but not an exciting boy, and young Arthur Stanley in 1828 probably describes what everyone felt about him: "I talked to William Gladstone almost all the time about all sorts of things. He is so very good-natured, and I like him very much. He talked a great deal about Eton, and said it was a very good place for those who liked boating and Latin verses. I think from what he said, I might get to like it." But as Stanley detested both boating and Latin verses, it is perhaps fortunate that he fell into the clutches of Dr. Arnold.

The same virtuous and exasperating dullness hangs over Gladstone's Oxford days. From October 1828 to 1831 he was in residence at Christ Church, formed an essay society called the W.E.G., and after a course of blameless study was rewarded with a double first. To the end of his life Gladstone insisted that undergraduates ought to work twelve hours a day! It was a bit early for the Oxford Movement, and Gladstone, faithful to his Evangelical upbringing, "abhorred the doctrine of baptismal regeneration." Only rather later, on May 13th, 1831, in the streets of Naples, did he grasp the significance of the Church. "You may smile," he said long after, "when told that when I was at Oxford Dr. Hampden was regarded as a model of orthodoxy; that Dr. Newman was eyed with suspicion as a low Churchman and Dr. Pusey as leaning to rationalism." The characteristic of Oxford religion, repulsive to the Liverpool Evangelical, was "a steady, clear, but dry Anglican orthodoxy" which "frowned this way or that, on the first indication of any tendency to diverge from the beaten path." So much for the "ancient University of Oxford, the God-fearing and God-sustaining University of Oxford," to which his final pieties returned, and which he thus addressed in a dying message.

But there was something else for Gladstone at Oxford, besides Bishop Butler and Aristotle and the steady, clear, but dry Anglican orthodoxy – the Oxford Union, that nursery of statesmen and hot-house for precocious rhetoric. From 1828 to 1831 the storm was blowing up for the Reform Bill, and Gladstone, " bred under the shadow of the great name of Canning,"[1] delivered a terrific onslaught for three-quarters of an hour on the principles of the Bill, though acute listeners asserted that he used Radical arguments the whole way through. When he sat down, " we all of us felt that an epoch of our lives had occurred." William was now in a great state of excitement (the highlander had for the moment emerged), and on his endeavouring to follow up his first speech with his first pamphlet, the lowland father protested. " I go with you in the main," he said, " but I cannot go all your lengths."

This ferocious outburst was to decide the next sixty-seven years of Gladstone's troubled existence. He did not rush light-heartedly into politics. On the contrary, he tortured himself with that meticulous conscientiousness which was always typical of him. He sincerely desired to go into the Church. And in a sense it did not matter what he did; for he was bound to be successful in whatever he undertook. As a clergyman, he would inevitably have become Primate; as a lawyer, Lord Chancellor. In earlier days he might have been a great Cardinal. But a politician he was to be. His friend, Lord Lincoln,

[1] Second reading of the 1866 Reform Bill.

recommended him to his father, the Duke of Newcastle, and he took his seat in the first reformed Parliament as member for the Duke's borough of Newark. One cannot but deplore this fact. Like his mentor Peel, the virtuous Harrow boy, who was also a double first at Christ Church, Gladstone got into the House before he had ever had time to think. How much time and trouble might not both Gladstone and Peel have saved themselves had they had to knock about the world a bit first, like the young Disraeli! Still, the rather backward young man of twenty-three could not behave quite correctly when standing for a ducal seat. His addresses were perfectly sound on the Union of the Church and State and "the defence in particular of our Irish establishment." But the Duke was much startled by a passage about "labour receiving adequate remuneration, which unhappily among several classes of our countrymen is not now the case." Gladstone had early formed his lifelong habit of sticking pins into his supporters. Further, although in this address he had, while desiderating proper Church instruction for the West India slaves, opposed emancipation till this instruction had fitted them for liberty, his father would never permit him to go and study his Jamaica plantations on the spot. Evidently he had seen from the start that there was something not quite safe about his wonderful William.

Once in the House, Gladstone "went all

lengths," but in the dreariest possible direction. His first vote was given against O'Connell's motion for repeal of the Union, and the next in favour of a stiff coercion bill; he then voted against the admission of Jews to Parliament, or of Dissenters to the University without a test; he supported the existing Corn Law and the houses and window taxes. He voted against the property tax, against the abolition of military and naval sinecures, and against the abolition of flogging in the navy save for mutiny and drunkenness; against the publication of division lists, against shorter Parliaments, and against the ballot. Particularly he spoke and voted against the gradual abolition of Colonial slavery and the reform of the Irish Church. Presumably, if you intend to box the compass, you might as well do it as thoroughly as possible. But such assiduity in wrongdoing, especially when combined with an infinite capacity for inventing pretexts, is never without its reward. Gladstone became Under-Secretary for the Colonies in the short administration of Sir Robert Peel, and was able to find in his new leader a partial substitute for his original hero Canning. The line along which he was to develop was now fixed; and also, he was fortunate in his office. For in Colonial matters, if in nothing else, Gladstone was always advanced.

It is a relief to turn away from Parliament, and the narrow efforts of the Tory Party to hold back Whig reforms already half a century overdue, to

Oxford, where the "steady, clear, but dry Anglican orthodoxy" was having the shock of its life. Gladstone's vision in the streets of Naples had now brightened marvellously, and he was rapidly unloading the whole cargo of Evangelicanism which he had shipped at Liverpool. "The suppression [by the Government] of ten Irish bishoprics, in defiance of Church opinion, showed how ready the Government was to take liberties in a high-handed way with the old adjustments of the relations of Church and State."[1] On July 14th, 1833, Keble preached the assize sermon in the University pulpit. It was published under the title of *National Apostasy*. "I have ever," wrote Newman, "considered and kept the day as the start of the religious movement of 1833."[2] The man who was finally to destroy the Irish establishment threw himself into the fray with a fine excitement. Here was a subject about which he could feel with his whole soul, and, though he was again to box the whole compass from theocracy to disestablishment, he had lighted upon an enthusiasm which was never to wane; which was to lead him to his first resignation and to his representation in Parliament of Oxford University, to make him the guardian of the perfect and free Episcopal Church of Scotland, to quarrel with the Protestants over the Catholic episcopacy in England, and with the Catholics over Infallibility,

[1] Church, *The Oxford Movement*, p. 82.
[2] Newman, *Apologia*, ed. 1927, p. 136.

which made him, stiff Churchman as he was, the liberator of ungrateful Nonconformity, which induced him to lay his hands on the establishment in Ireland and on the establishment in Wales, to bring down his Government of 1868 in an endeavour to set up a Catholic University in Ireland, and to stand forth everywhere as the defender of religious freedom. The band of Oxford dons in the Oriel Common Room, had they been blessed with powers of prophecy, would have pushed aside in horror this Greek arriving with his gifts. During the ten years of Whig ascendancy his heart was more in Oxford than in Westminster, and in 1838 he published his first book, *The Church Considered in its Relations with the State*, the book that led Macaulay to describe the author as the " last hope of the stern unbending Tories " and to enquire mockingly, " Why not roast Dissenters in front of slow fires ? " This book is interesting as another proof of the author's willingness to " go all lengths," even to suggesting that the Church of England is alone the repository of truth and should force everyone into its mould. We must remember this first work, which was to lead to the author's first resignation.

The time not given to the Oxford Movement was devoted to courtship and marriage. In the winter of 1838 Gladstone had " arrived at an understanding " in Sicily with Miss Catherine Glynne, and on July 25th, 1839, the marriage took place at Hawarden, the property of the bride's brother, Sir Stephen Glynne, who by the unwearying vigilance, it is said, of Mrs. Gladstone, lived and died unmarried. Hawarden was heavily encumbered. Gladstone paid off some £100,000 of mortgage, and thus eventually became owner of that famous property, which in the minds of many people stood as a rival to Windsor, a nineteenth-century counterpart to Chanteloup.[1] Gladstone's engagement to a physical object as healthy and resistant as himself was not completely easy. He proposed, suitably enough, in the Colosseum. The lady hesitated, as she was suffering from an emotional disappointment. "I have only half a heart to offer," she protested. "Give it to me and I will make it a whole one," was the exquisitely sensitive retort. He had his way, and the magnificent male led off the magnificent female to the marriage bed, which they were to share for sixty years, as fine a couple as ever faced life together. With Mrs. Gladstone in his hand, and with Hawarden in the offing, the background of his existence was now complete, save for the large noisy family which was to racket among the Wellingtonias in the park.

By 1841 the Melbourne administration was tottering to its doom amid the execrations of the Chartists and in a welter of unbalanced budgets. The General Election of 1841 decided that Sir Robert Peel was to gain the reward for the

[1] Gladstone said with academic humour of Hawarden Park that "it was not in the first class, but was high up in the second class."

education he had been inflicting on his party, and in August the Minister was collecting together one of the most gifted administrations that have ever held office in England. The young Gladstone was again marked out for office. Indeed, everyone had begun taking an interest in him. Lord Malmesbury was delighted at his opportunity of meeting Gladstone, quite one of the rising men, though he was disappointed in his appearance, which reminded him of a Roman Catholic ecclesiastic. Peel showed he knew the capacities of his young recruit better than he knew them himself, when he offered him the Vice-Presidentship of the Board of Trade. As the main work of the Ministry was to be financial reform and the President, Lord Ripon – shortly to retire – was a cipher, this apparently subordinate post was among the most important in the Government. To the outside world, Gladstone at the age of thirty-two seemed about to enter on a career of sober office, in the manner of Peel, whom he superficially so much resembled. That he was not in the least like Peel was a discovery reserved for a later date.

As it seems now obvious that this son of a Liverpool shipowner, who had passed his boyish holidays amid the bustle of the shipyards and who was to become the greatest Budget-maker of the nineteenth century, was intended by nature for the Board of Trade, Peel has not got the credit he deserves for the imaginative skill of the appointment. For Gladstone, far from springing a financial Athene from the head of Pluto, had never apparently bestowed a moment's attention on problems of commerce. His whole adult life had been devoted to religion, and he had already been irritated by his political friends' indifference to his book on Church and State. In a quarter of an hour's conversation with Peel he insisted that "I am not really fit for it. I have no general knowledge of trade whatever : with a few questions I am acquainted, but they are such as have come across me incidentally," and in an autobiographical note of a later date he returns to the subject :

"I was totally ignorant of political economy and of the commerce of the country. I might have said, as I believe was said by a former holder of the vice-presidency, that my mind was in regard to all these matters 'a sheet of white paper,' except that it was doubtless coloured by a traditional prejudice of Protection which had then quite recently become a distinctive mark of Conservatism. In a spirit of ignorant mortification I said to myself at the moment : The science of politics deals with the Government of men, but I am set to govern packages. In my journal for August 2nd I find this recorded : 'Since the address meetings (which were quasi-cabinets) the idea of the Irish Secretaryship had nestled imperceptibly in my mind.'"

This note reveals completely the difference between Gladstone and Peel. At no moment in

Peel's life would he have made such a distinction between men and packages. And at this entry into his heritage Gladstone must have cast his eye back, though perhaps for the last time, in regret for the clerical profession and a stall at Christ Church amid the warm familiar conflicts of the Oxford Movement. Fortunately for his subsequent comfort, his Puseyite tendencies prevented his becoming Irish Secretary in 1841. The Ulster Presbyterians would not have liked it. Later they were to dislike other things still more.

Still, it was never Gladstone's nature to skimp a job, however distasteful. He set himself to master the packages and do the donkey work for Peel's series of devastating Budgets. He soon shed his traditional prejudice of Protection and grappled so furiously with the mass of petty tariffs that in May 1843 he entered the Cabinet as President of the Board. He was the greatest success in the Government. Peel began to rely on him for everything and he in return to show how extremely irritating he could be. The question of the Corn Laws was exasperating Peel, whose conscience could no longer consent to their present condition. Three courses were open : a low fixed duty, a sliding scale based on the world price, or immediate abolition. Gladstone, though he had originally wanted to travel faster than Peel, saw grave objections to all three courses. Even Peel, the most patient of men, was ruffled. He was just beginning to realise that Gladstone, a master of detail and lucid statement, was, by some psychological necessity, frequently compelled to wrap up everything in a fog of qualifications, and so lead many intelligent people to say that he was nothing but a sophistical time-server.[1] But mere quibbling about the incidence of the Corn Law was as nothing to the annoyances which were to follow. Peel's front bench was already weakening in debate, when Gladstone found it necessary to resign on a point which would have troubled no one else. Peel intended to embark on a large programme of Irish reform, and wished, as a beginning, to increase the annual grant to the Irish clerical college of Maynooth, agreed to at the time of the Union. This grant to error was inconsistent with what Gladstone had said in his book on Church and State, and he handed in his resignation. He no longer believed what he had said in his book and was hopeful that when he saw the proposition he would be able to support it. But what would be thought of the honour of public men if they attacked things in books which they then supported in office, without the public having been first notified of a change of opinion? A hideous suspicion would hang over the motives of members of Parliament. Peel simply could not understand such a conscience, and, as Gladstone's style grew increasingly obscure with his excitement

[1] Gladstone's love of qualification could on occasion become maniacal. "It is within the power of every man to make money by breeding poultry, and, if I may say so, from eggs" (address to the tenants of Hawarden in 1884).

(and only under strong excitement could he have resigned at such an important moment in his career), he was quite unable to express himself intelligibly to his chief, who wrote in considerable anger to Sir James Graham :

January 3rd : " I really have great difficulty sometimes in comprehending what Gladstone means. I take it for granted, however, that his letter means to announce his continued intention to retire . . . and I greatly regret it. . . . Is it not strange that this letter marked ' Secret ' – and being secret if ever letter was – came to me this morning by post *open* ? It may have been read in every post office through which it has passed."

Graham replied the next day :

" It is always difficult through the haze of words to catch a distant glimpse of Gladstone's meaning. But though the letter is obscure, the resolution, I am afraid, is taken, and you must consider the note as an announcement that if we proceed with our Maynooth measure he will retire.

" Gladstone's omission to seal such a letter was most unfortunate : but the enigmatic style has its advantages. I doubt whether there is a postmaster in England who after reading the letter would understand one word of it."[1]

Nor was the retiring Minister more fortunate in his explanations to a larger public. Greville notes in his diary for February 6th : " Gladstone's explanation was ludicrous. Everybody said that he had only succeeded in showing that his resignation was quite uncalled-for."

However, " All's well that ends well." Gladstone having resigned on the Maynooth grant,

[1] Parker, *Life of Sir James Graham*, Vol. II., p. 2.

and then voted for the Maynooth grant, was ready to take office again, and in December 1845 he was installed in the Colonial Department, when the failure of the Irish potato crop was making the immediate repeal of the Corn Laws inevitable. Unfortunately, the Duke of Newcastle did not see the necessity for this economic revolution, and Gladstone lost his first seat. So, though a Cabinet Minister, he was without a seat, and did not sit by Peel during the famous division which overthrew his Government (taken nominally on an Irish Coercion Bill and on the very evening that the Corn Bill passed through the Lords), when the Tories split the Tory Party on a subject which was worth a split – on the final struggle between the old England and the new, and when, in the famous words of Disraeli, " the Manners, the Somersets, the Bentincks, the Lowthers, and the Lennoxes passed before him [Peel] . . . if his heart were hardened to Sir Charles Burrell, Sir William Joliffe, Sir Charles Knightly, Sir John Trollope, Sir Edward Kerrison, Sir John Tyrill, he surely must have had a pang when his eye rested on Sir John Yarde Buller, his choice and pattern country gentleman, whom he himself had selected and invited some six years back to move a vote of want of confidence in the Whig Government, in order, against the feeling of the court, to install Sir Robert Peel in their stead.

" They trooped on: all the men of mettle, the large-acred squires, whose spirit he had so often quickened and whose council he had so often solicited in his fine Conservative speeches in Whitehall Gardens: Mr. Banks with a parliamentary name of two centuries, and Mr. Christopher from that broad Lincolnshire which Protection had created: and the Mileses and the Henleys were there: and the Duncombes and the Liddells and the Yorkes. And Devon had sent there the stout heart of Mr. Buck, and Wiltshire the pleasant presence of Walter Long. . . . The news that the Government was not only beaten, but by a majority so large as 73, began to circulate. An incredulous murmur passed along the Treasury Bench . . . [Sir Robert] began to comprehend his position and that the Emperor was without his army."[1]

The first stage of Gladstone's life was over. For the next thirteen years he was to spend but some two in office.

[1] Disraeli, *Life of Lord George Bentinck*, pp. 299–301.

CHAPTER II

The thirteen years' interregnum – Don Pacifico and foreign policy – papal oppression and religious policy – Gladstone's first Budget and financial policy – the reform of Oxford University and the Civil Service – the Crimean War and resignation of Gladstone – Prolonged isolation.

THE Reform Bill of 1832, the Tory split over the Corn Law, and the Liberal split over Home Rule were the three most important events in nineteenth-century Parliamentary history, but the Corn Law split introduced a confusion which did not attend the other two revolutions, and which made the next twenty years sterile. The Corn Laws, once destroyed, could not possibly be revived. The constituencies had with a doubtful voice ratified a decision dictated with an angry roar by the voteless adherents of the Corn Law League. The Tories had been compelled to abandon their beliefs, and the Whigs had no beliefs to offer on their own account. Thus the House turned into a huge debating society bombinating in a vacuum. Save for the all-important Ten Hours Act passed under the Whig Government in 1847 and the Navigation Acts of '49 and '54, the impotence of Parliament is only relieved by the squalid interlude of the Crimean War and the nightmare of the Mutiny. Time unending was wasted over the proposal and rejection of petty reform Bills. The terms £10 freeholders, £8 freeholders, £6 freeholders, and compound freeholders dominate a succession of Parliaments, which were unable to decide whether 150,000 or 200,000 voters could be safely added to the electoral body. The remnants of the Peel Faction, the Conservative Free Traders, the *état-major sans armée*, controlled and paralysed Parliaments rather as the remnants of the Liberal Party have done in our own day. The battle raged round personalities – the personalities of Palmerston and Disraeli. Unfortunately, both personalities were equally distasteful to the Peelites, Palmerston for his jingoism and Disraeli for the brutal energy and virulent dialectic with which he had destroyed Peel and raised himself into the vacant leadership. At any moment after 1846 Gladstone could have raised himself into office. It would not have been difficult to come to terms with the Whigs. Disraeli twice with great abnegation offered to surrender the leadership of the Tories. After the death of Peel in 1850, Gladstone nearly controlled the House with his bundle of followers, but was apparently seized with an inhibition. He could destroy Governments but could not form them, and so became a sort of English Clemenceau. The situation continued till he quite suddenly made the decision he might have made years before, and joined the Whig Cabinet of 1859. These thirteen years spent searching for a party form an extraordinary interlude in the life of a man who seemed made for office, and who later in life did indeed appear to regard the formation of a Cabinet by Mr. Gladstone as part of the providential scheme of things. Personal antipathy both to Palmerston and Disraeli was certainly the cause of his indecision.

When the new Parliament met after the General Election of 1846, Gladstone was junior member for Oxford University, the "Liberal" burgess in the academic sense, the Conservative interests of the place being looked after by his trusted old colleague, Sir Robert Inglis. The residents, the heads of houses, and the double firsts, with a fair sprinkling of Puseyites, voted for Gladstone, the rank and file of the electorate for Inglis. Gladstone was immensely flattered by an election which had in it a certain fitness, and which gave him a certain dignity. But nevertheless it was unfortunate, and hampered his development. He was always in danger of losing a seat to which he attached a sentimental importance. Secondly, the inspired platform-speaker, who could sway masses of opinion as no one before or since, found himself member for a constituency that could not be addressed. He thus was cut off entirely from the exercise of his greatest talent, and he rarely addressed a public meeting till the 'sixties. No estimate of Gladstone can be sound which does not insist on the difficulties he accumulated in the way of his own advancement.

But it was in this 1846 Parliament, when the Peelites, out of hatred of Disraeli, kept in office a Government they detested almost as much, that

Gladstone learned to dominate the chamber as he learned later to dominate the constituencies.

On June 27th, 1850, took place the famous debate on Don Pacifico (it was the last occasion on which Peel addressed the House), when Palmerston was attacked for having sent British ships of war to the Piræus as a protest against the refusal of Greece to compensate excessively Don Pacifico (a Maltese Jew and British subject) for losses suffered during a riot in Athens. Palmerston triumphed in a speech lasting " from the dusk of one day till the dawn of the next,"[1] but, when the noise was over, Gladstone had enlisted the sympathy of all decent people. The whole speech was a protest against Palmerston's habit of bullying the weak and truckling to the strong, and can be read to-day with perfect satisfaction. But one passage is a particularly good specimen of that elaborate irony which stood Gladstone in place of the more obvious wit:

" But, Sir, without resorting to a single hostile testimony the papers presented to me on the part of M. Pacifico contain in my judgment too many presumptions of the same kind. And though his being a Jew is not a reason for debarring him of any of his just rights, yet neither is it a reason for exempting him from enquiry to which other persons would be subjected, irrespectively of their creed, under similar circumstances. Now I ask the question whether anyone in this House has

[1] This is the famous " Civis romanus sum " speech.

read the celebrated inventory of M. Pacifico's furniture and effects without finding it bears on the face of it all the proofs of gross, palpable and wilful exaggeration? It is declared by Baron Gros, in language by no means too strong, to be a 'deplorable exaggeration.' It recites the value of the articles of his furniture: and then the learned member for Bath [Sir Alexander Cockburn] thinks that he has solved the difficulty by telling us that he has been to some upholsterer in London, who said he could easily make a couch worth £170 or even more. This is rare simplicity. Yes! no doubt many a London upholsterer could make a couch worth £170, and could get him a chest of drawers worth £53, a carpet worth £60, a card table worth £24, two mirrors worth £120, and a bed worth £150 and so forth: no doubt he could also purchase at shops in London of another class a china dinner service worth £170 and two tea and coffee services worth £64. All these could be bought in London: you may find such articles in shops; and you may find some of them in private mansions, but then they are found inside the houses of men who outside those houses have £20,000, £50,000 or £100,000 of income by the year. Then again you find recited as having been in the house of M. Pacifico all these articles and many more besides of the same high relative values, and the very first thing that must occur to a reader of the catalogue and strike him as utterly marvellous is, that he not only has the finest furniture and finest clothes in his house, but no other kind of clothes or furniture. There was not an ordinary article of either from the top to the bottom of the house. Everything in it was a specimen of the richest and rarest of its kind. When I first heard this statement made in another place, I confess I thought it must have been a figure of rhetorical licence; and the house cannot now learn with more surprise than I did, when I examined the document for myself, that the whole appliances and appointments of the mansion of Pacifico were characterised by this astonishing luxury. And yet this man, who thus surpassed nearly all subjects and equalled almost any prince, according to his own account, in many articles of luxury, who has £5,000 worth of clothes, jewels and furniture in his house, had not outside of it, except plate pledged to the Bank of Athens for £30, which he had not been able to redeem, one single farthing! The subject of M. Pacifico's claims may be a tedious one to the House, it has been so frequently under their notice; but I venture to express the opinion that the details of them, as they are contained in these volumes, would really afford no bad material for some ingenious writer of romance.

"So, Sir, having his house crammed full of fine furniture, fine clothes, and fine jewels, M. Pacifico was in all other respects a pauper. But this is not all: it is plain that his furniture, as he described it, was massive and solid in the highest degree.

And yet we are told of its disappearing, of its being broken to pieces and destroyed. It is not pretended that fire was used, but that a mob came into his house and in an hour and a half, or, according to other places in the book, three hours, destroyed these solid masses of mahogany. Why, Sir, they could not without fire have destroyed such articles, unless indeed they had eaten them. Sir, the whole statement bears upon the face of it outrageous fraud and falsehood. A man with this large mass of property in his house carries on the trade of a moneylender upon a borrowed capital of £30, and, when this furniture is destroyed, declares that he has not an *obolus* wherewith to buy his bread. No such case ever existed."

But the year 1850 was not to pass away before the country was involved in another outburst of John Bullishness – scarcely more creditable than the affair of Don Pacifico – which Gladstone was again to acquire unpopularity for opposing. The Church was still " reeling " from the defection of Dr. Newman ; a large number of Oxford and Mayfair conversions to Rome had taken place, and, grotesque as it now appears, many sensible persons seriously thought that Protestant England was about to throw over the Reformation and, taper in hand, follow barefooted friars through the streets of Birmingham and Manchester. The Papacy not unnaturally decided to take an active part in the " Movement." About the month of October a most unfortunately worded document, written "from without the Flaminian Gate," appeared under the name of the new Cardinal Archbishop of Westminster, Dr. Wiseman. One paragraph was particularly unhappy in its phrasing:

"By a brief appointed the same day his Holiness was pleased to appoint us, though most unworthy, to the Archiepiscopal See of Westminster, established by the above-mentioned letters apostolic, giving us at the same time the administration of the Episcopal See of Southwark. So that, at present and till such time as the Holy See shall think fit otherwise to provide, we govern and shall continue to govern the Counties of Middlesex, Hertford, and Essex, as Ordinary thereof, and those of Surrey, Sussex, Kent, Berkshire, and Hampshire, with the Islands annexed, as administrator with ordinary jurisdiction."

This pursy, clerical paragraph meant nothing save that territorial titles were to be added to existing administrations. Frenzy, however, settled upon the public, whose dreams were poisoned once more by the spectacle of olive-faced padres from Spain in control of Durham stalls. The Prime Minister, Lord John Russell, stimulated the prevailing excitement with a hysterical letter published on the eve of Guy Fawkes' Day to the Bishop of Durham, and amid thunders of applause the Lord Chancellor (Truro) at the Mansion House quoted the lines:

> "Under our feet we'll stamp thy Cardinal's hat,
> In spite of Pope or dignities of Church."

Ferocious statements were uttered by the Episcopal Bench, all the bishops except two uniting in an address to the Queen which described the Pope's act as an unwarrantable insult. *The Times*, with the other newspapers, followed suit. In private, however, the editor thought the whole thing merely good copy. "Delane, who begged me not to write," notes Greville, "as I was inclined to do, something in mitigation of the movement, told me he thought the whole thing gross humbug and a pack of nonsense." Amid general approval Lord John introduced a Bill fining anyone who used the titles £100. The second reading was passed by 438 votes to 95. One third of the minority was Irish and the rest included every intelligent member of the House of Commons off the Treasury Bench. Gladstone's contribution to the debate was a fitting pendant to his speech on Don Pacifico, giving, as it did, his whole attitude on home affairs. He skilfully based his appeal on the needless fear of Rome shown by a great country.

"Show, I beseech you, have the courage to show, the Pope of Rome and his Cardinals and his Church that England too, as well as Rome, has her *semper eadem*: and that when she has once adopted some great principle of legislation, which is destined to influence the national character, to draw the dividing-lines of her policy for ages to come, and to affect the whole nature of her standing among the nations of the world, show that when once she has done this slowly, and done this deliberately, she has done it once for all, and that she will then no more retrace her steps than the river which bathes this giant city can flow back upon its source. The character of England is in our hands. Let us feel the responsibility that belongs to us and let us rely on it. If to-day we make this step backwards, it is one which hereafter we shall have to retrace with pain. We cannot change the profound and resistless tendencies of the age towards religious liberty. It is our business to control and to guide their application. . . . We are in a minority insignificant in point of numbers. We are more insignificant still because we are but knots and groups of two or three; we have no powers of cohesion, no bonds of union. What is it that binds us together against you but the conviction that we have on our side the principle of justice – the conviction that we shall soon have on our side the strength of public opinion?" The Ecclesiastical Titles Bill, with its penal clauses cut out, passed triumphantly through both Houses, to become an immediate dead letter, and to be repealed by Gladstone in 1871. In a few weeks it was obvious that Lord John had done nothing except weaken his Government by offending the Irish members.

But the lesson of religious toleration is the hardest and most civilised of lessons, and is always having to be learned afresh. In 1883, Gladstone, at the height of his power and in possession of a large majority, was to be again defeated on a similar question, the Affirmation Bill, a measure to permit free thinkers, in the person of Bradlaugh, to "affirm" instead of taking the oath "So help me, God." While the Government was losing one by-election after another because they "supported atheists," Gladstone, now seventy-four years old, was still hard at work, arguing away as he had argued in 1850.

"Let us try to get at the heart of the argument, which after all is not a very complex, although I must say it is historically, and from every point of view a very interesting matter. The business of every man in controversy is to try to find out what is the main and governing contention of his adversary. Sir, I have laboured to find that out and I think I have probably found it : I hope so. As I read it the governing contention is this – that the main question for the State is not what religion a man professes, but whether he professes some religion or none. I was in the hopes of receiving some confirmatory testimony for the other side. I might dispense with proofs, but I will give them. The right honourable gentleman who led the opposition to this Bill said that this was not a question of difference of religion, but that it was a question between religion and irreligion – between religion and the absence of all religion – and clearly the basis of the right hon. gentleman's speech was not that we were to tolerate any belief, but that we were not to tolerate no belief. . . . My hon. friend the member for Finsbury still more clearly expressed similar views. He referred to the ancient controversies as all very well: they touched, he said, excrescences, and not the vital substance. Now, Sir, I want to examine what is the vital substance and what are the excrescences. He went further than this and used a most apt, appropriate, expressive, and still more significant phrase. He said, 'Yes, it is true you may admit religions, some of which go near the precipice; but now you ask us to go over it.' Gentlemen opposite cheered loudly when that was said by the hon. gentleman behind me. They will not give me a single cheer now. They suspect I am quoting this with some evil intent. The question is, am I quoting them fairly? Or is it the fact that some gentlemen have not fully and fairly considered their relations to the present Bill, except that they mean to oppose whatever proceeds from the Government? But my hon. friend has considered very well what he said when he used the remarkable simile about the precipice. I wish to see what is the value of this main and principal contention – this doctrine of the precipice – this question between religion and irreligion, between some belief which is to be tolerated and no belief which cannot be tolerated. . . . The hon. and learned gentleman the member for Launceston . . . adopted a phrase which had fallen from the hon. member for Portsmouth [Sir H. Drummond

Wolff] . . . and he said he wished there should be some form of belief and some recognition of belief – something of what is called in philosophical discussion the recognition of the supernatural. That I believe is a phrase that goes as near to what the hon. gentlemen opposite mean as anything can. It is the existence at any rate of the supernatural that is wanted. That is the main contention of the party opposite, and what I want to know is, whether that contention – that proposition – offers us as a good solid standing ground for legislation ? "

The House, however, refused to be impinged on the horns of Gladstone's dilemmas and the Bill was rejected by three votes. Like Lord John Russell, Gladstone was opposed by the weight of the Irish members. Few people believe in liberty for anyone except themselves. Gladstone, with all his limitations, belonged to the respectable minority which understands that liberty does not merely mean freedom to trample on one's neighbours.

The Government of Lord John Russell, incapable of devising anything except reform Bills which nobody wanted, died of hemorrhage, and was succeeded by the first of the Conservative minority Governments in which Disraeli was Chancellor of the Exchequer and leader of the House of Commons. After a General Election in which the Conservative Party, though improving its position, did not attain a majority, the Peelites – that is to say, Gladstone – still controlled the

House. Disraeli introduced a Budget, a rather half-baked measure containing valuable hints for future finance, particularly the distinction between earned and unearned income as a basis for taxation. Gladstone destroyed the proposals, and a prolonged political crisis followed, to end in the formation of a coalition Cabinet in which the Peelite minority, led by Aberdeen, seized on all the best offices, the others being divided among the Whigs and one Radical. This was the Ministry which " drifted " into the Crimean War. Its active achievement was the Budget of 1853, the first ever to be introduced by Gladstone.

Gladstone's Budgets were not intended to be merely methods of raising revenue : they fell into a general scheme of politics, and give the clue to his whole view of the relations of the individual to the State ; so it may be as well at this point to give a general conspectus of his contribution to finance. One idea ran through all his Budgets and he did not achieve his end. In finance, as in many other matters, his desires were frustrated by circumstance.

He had one main principle – economy. Economy was for him a passion, not, as for Peel, merely a form of good housekeeping. The less money a Government had the better, for it was probably spent very badly – especially on armaments and every form of jingoism. To keep down expenditure was his first principle. And, as national expenditure was a bad thing, taxes were bad things too. To all forms of protection Gladstone was opposed: and his Budgets of 1859 to 1863 were devoted to freeing commerce to its ultimate extent. Here he finished off the work of Huskisson in the 'twenties and of Peel in the 'forties. He made no great palaver as to the rival merits of direct and indirect taxation. They both had their uses. Addressing the house in 1861 on this point, he expressed himself as follows:

"I can never think of direct or indirect taxation except as I should think of two attractive sisters, who have been introduced into the gay world of London; each with an ample fortune: both having the same parentage (for the parents of both I believe to be necessity and invention), differing only as sisters may differ, as where one is of a lighter and another of a darker complexion, or where there is some agreeable variety of manner, the one being free and open, and the other somewhat more shy, retiring, and insinuating. I cannot conceive why there should be unfriendly rivalry between the admirers of these two damsels, and I frankly own, whether it be due to a lax sense of moral indignation or not, that as Chancellor of the Exchequer, if not as a member of this House, I have always thought it not only allowable, but even an act of duty, to pay my addresses to them both."

But here Gladstone was being unusually gallant. His normal attitude towards both these interesting débutantes was one of suspicion and dislike. In his first Budget he drew up an ideal scheme of income tax for seven years.

"Our proposition, then, so far as it merely regards the income tax, is this: We propose to renew it for two years from April 1853 at the rate of 7*d.* in the £. The Committee will recollect that I said that we thought it our duty to look the whole breadth of this difficulty in the face: not to endeavour to escape it, not to endeavour to attenuate or to understate it, but to face and to settle it, if the Committee would enable us – the whole question of the income tax. We propose, then, to enact it for two years from April '53 to April '55 at the rate of 7*d.* in the £; from April '55 to enact it for two more years at 6*d.* in the £; and then for three years more – I cannot wonder at the smile which I perceive my words provoke – for three years more – from April '57 – at 5*d.* Under this proposal, on April 5th, 1860, the income tax will expire."

This scheme was wrecked in the following year by the Crimean War.

Let us now take up the subject again in 1859 at the point when Gladstone became for fifteen years the financial master of England. In 1859, as in 1853, he found himself faced with a deficit; and, though still theoretically opposed to the income tax, he promptly raised it from 3*d.* to 9*d.*, all to be raised in the first half of the year, thus providing the surplus for his "golden" Budget of 1861. By the time Gladstone resigned office in 1874, he had reduced the income tax to 3*d.*; and he promised, if re-elected to power, to abolish it altogether and thus fulfil the pledge given in 1853. But the newly enfranchised working classes, to Gladstone's naïve surprise, saw no reasons why the middle classes should not pay income tax, and returned Disraeli in his place. The next year, indeed, the income tax was reduced to 2*d.*; but it never showed any sign of going lower, and Gladstone accepted the result of the election as a considered verdict of the constituencies in favour of a permanent income tax. Since then it has done scarcely anything but rise, and has become the engine for effecting a revolution in political technique. Economy, instead of being something beautiful, virginal, and passionate, has become the symbol of cowardice and stagnation. The system of "robbing Peter to pay Paul" became the doctrine of Radicalism, practised in its full beauty under the Asquith administration, and upon which Labour Governments have as yet been unable to improve. Gladstone's views on the philosophy of the State have not prevailed.

But for one purpose the income tax was very much to Gladstone's taste. It could always be useful to damp enthusiasm in time of war. He opposed financing wars out of loans, and, with the naïveté characteristic of this most subtle mind, blurted out his thoughts on his Budget speech in 1854 just before the outbreak of the Crimean

War, when he doubled the income tax for the first half of the year.

" The expenses of war are a moral check, which it has pleased the Almighty to impose upon the ambition and lust of conquest that are inherent in so many nations. There is pomp and circumstance, there is glory and excitement about war which, notwithstanding the miseries it entails, invests it with charm in the eyes of the community, and tends to blind man to those evils to a fearful and dangerous degree. The necessity of meeting from year to year the expenditure which it entails is a salutary and wholesome check, making them feel what they are about and making them measure the cost of the benefit upon which they may calculate. It is by these means that they may be led and brought to address themselves to a war policy as rational and intelligent beings, and may be induced to keep their eyes well fixed upon the necessity of the war into which they are about to enter, and their determination of availing themselves of the first and earliest prospects of concluding an honourable peace."

This was thought no fit way for the Chancellor of the Exchequer in a war cabinet to speak. " Moreover, only a few weeks later, when affairs became more serious, Gladstone himself was compelled to borrow on Exchequer bonds in anticipation of taxes. But he showed no lack of courage or promptitude in meeting the growing demands of the war : for on May 8th he produced another

Budget providing for the continuance of the income tax at the doubled rate of 1*s.* 2*d.* in the £ till the close of war. Moreover, by adding to the duties on spirits and malt, he raised enough revenue (£6,850,000) to cover the enlarged estimates of expenditure and leave his original surplus undisturbed."[1] So far Mr. Gladstone on the punitive merits of taxation.

The first three Budgets of the 'sixties rounded off the work of Peel by the abolition of the timber duties, the abolition of the paper duties, and the abolition of the remaining taxes on manufactured articles, which was our contribution to the commercial treaty with France, arranged by Cobden and inserted with immense skill into the Budget, so that it was impossible to reject one without rejecting the other. The commercial treaty with France had an immense effect on foreign policy, which can be properly treated elsewhere. The question of the paper duties was also as much political as economic. It was thought that cheap paper would permit the working classes to acquire undesirable information, and, with the tacit approval of Lord Palmerston, the House of Lords rejected the Bill. Gladstone reintroduced it the next year, sending up all his financial proposals in one Bill ; so that the Lords could only reject but could no longer amend a Budget. The Lords gave way, and did not again tamper with a finance Bill till 1909. In 1853 also Gladstone

[1] Hirst, *Gladstone as Financier and Economist*, p. 160.

introduced the succession duty, which extended to successions in real property duties similar to those payable in the case of legacies. He hoped shortly to raise £2,000,000 a year by this method ; in effect, he was only raising £600,000 a year by 1860, and the miscalculation damaged in the late 'fifties Gladstone's reputation as a financier.

To modern ideas Gladstone's finance appears unadventurous and middle-class, the least interesting of his achievements. "We are all socialists now," remarked Sir William Harcourt, and Gladstone's directly opposing point of view is perhaps unsuitable for the management of large modern societies. He at any rate would have had to become a centenarian before he could have become a socialist. That it was the business of the Government to oppose demands from differing interests of the community remained a fixed principle with him, and he deplored the decay of this view among all sections of society. In this he agreed with Queen Victoria :

> "The Queen cannot help feeling," she writes to Lord Granville in 1880, "uneasy at the state of the House of Commons. There is such an amount of interferences and meddling in everything, that, unless it is firmly resisted, government will become impossible. It would be grievous indeed and *very serious*, if this democratic spirit were *not checked* ; and the Queen thinks Mr. Gladstone has it in his power by his experience and influence as well as by his great majority to raise the tone and not let the House of Commons become as it were the executive power which is what this constant interference and constant questioning increasingly *leads to*. . . .

"It is the more necessary as so many office people like Mr. Chamberlain, Sir C. Dilke and Mr. Mundella and others, *themselves* very guilty of such proceedings, may *not* be *aware* of the necessity of checking such questions or of how to answer."

Gladstone, however, replied with exquisite subtlety:

"Undoubtedly . . . there has grown up, within the last quarter of a century, a most urgent tendency in Parliament to invade the office of the Executive Government, which invests it with the sole initiative in the matter of public charge. This tendency has been manifest in all sections of political party, but it has been beyond doubt, as Mr. Gladstone thinks, especially observable in what is termed the landed interest and in the Officers of the Army. It has brought about a large increase of the public expenditure: which setting aside the public debt, as matter of obligation and not of choice, is more than double now what it was thirty years ago: large portions of the increase being indubitably legitimate, or even necessary, but other portions representing the power of the interests of class, rather than the urgency of public wants. This tendency weakens the Government and lowers greatly the sense of responsibility in the House of Commons. . . . On this very evening, however, the first motion, by Earl Percy, aimed at disturbing anew the Abolition of Purchase (Commissions in the Army), to the prejudice of the nation; and the second by Mr. Leighton at the further lightening of the liabilities of the ratepayer, by a transfer of charge to the Exchequer; which certainly means in a greater or less degree casting upon labour burdens hitherto borne by property."

Thus Gladstone with immense cleverness succeeded in agreeing with the Queen in a sense contrary to what she had intended. And his ability to produce arguments more suitable to an Oxford Essay Society than to the royal boudoir no doubt tended to exacerbate his relations with a character as straightforward and unsophisticated as the Queen's.

Gladstone was of course not successful in opposing what was an irresistible tendency of the age, though, as undisputed head of the Radical Party, he perhaps succeeded in stabilising *laissez faire* beyond the point when *laissez faire* was serviceable to the community. It is, however, creditable equally to himself and the working classes that he succeeded in keeping their loyalty, when he had so little to offer save spiritual values. Further, the uses to which Europe has put the vast wealth extracted by the income tax is evidence that Gladstone had a good deal of wisdom on his side.

. . . .

The great Government of 1853 sank into despicable defeat with the Crimean War ; nor did Gladstone appear at his best during the negotiations which led up to it. It can be said in his favour that this was his first acquaintance with foreign policy ; that his hesitancies were shared by all his colleagues, and that he was right in objecting to Russia doing single-handed the work of the European Concert. However, in February 1855, when war was certain, he recounts an interview with Lord Aberdeen which one would rather had not taken place. After arguing correctly that the mere declaration of war does not make a defensive war offensive or vice versa, he stated that " to retire upon such a declaration would be to retire upon no ground warrantable and conceivable by reason. . . . He [Aberdeen] asked, how could he bring himself to fight for the Turks? I said we were not fighting for the Turks, but we were warning Russia off the forbidden ground. That, indeed, if we undertook to put down the Christians under Turkish rule by force, then we should be fighting for the Turks, but to this for one I could be no party. He said that if I saw a way for him to get out, he hoped that I should mention it. . . . [I said] that we were not going to extend the conflagration (but I had to correct myself as to the Baltic), but to apply more power for its extinction, and this, I hoped, in conjunction with all the great powers of Europe. That I for one could not *shoulder the musket* (!) against the Christian subjects of the Sultan, and must there take my stand."[1]

And so Gladstone drifted into the Crimean War. But, as Bright said, he always had a bad conscience about it, and it may have been this bad conscience which later made him so violent in the opposite direction.

Gladstone, however, might have avoided getting implicated in the Crimean War had he not been at this very moment carried away with enthusiasm about the Reform of Oxford University, now rendered inevitable by the report of the Commission set up by Lord John Russell in 1850. It is characteristic of Gladstone that he had violently

[1] Morley, Vol. I., p. 492.

opposed the setting up of such a commission as *ultra vires*, but that, when once it had reported, he threw himself with equal energy into the effecting of its recommendations. The fury of interest which this problem excited in him may be estimated from the fact that he preserved 560 letters and documents relating to the preparation and passing of the Oxford University Bill, and among them over 350 copies of his own letters between December 1853 and December 1854. The main result of this measure was to alter the government of the University, to free much money for general educational purposes, and, though still confining the teaching staff to the Church of England, to open degrees to Dissenters. As Chancellor of the Exchequer, Gladstone also supported the throwing open of the Civil Service to competitive examination, though nomination had first to be procured. He himself as Prime Minister rounded off both these reforms. It is extraordinary and perhaps undesirable that a Chancellor of the Exchequer, particularly when England is at war, should find time to take up a question as complicated as the Oxford University Bill, which he, to a great extent, drafted himself. It might have been a good thing had he kept his mind fixed on the general political situation. The condition of internal ferment in which he always lived was continually leading him to turn his attention away from one thing in order to concentrate on another, sometimes to the exclusion of more important matters. On occasion his passion would amount to an *idée fixe* ; and the public's inability to foresee what cause would next excite his enthusiasm engendered apprehension among his friends, rage among his opponents, and instability in the body politic. For his passions, though easily kindled, were with difficulty stifled. Only an immense output of energy could calm a nature as tenacious as it was erratic. Cynics and opponents might argue that these volte-face were due to a search for power. But Gladstone never feared to make himself unpopular, as he was to show in 1855, and it is remarkable that his sponsoring of University reform did not lose him his seat for Oxford in 1857.

The Aberdeen Government fell on a motion by Roebuck, demanding the setting up of a commission to enquire into the conduct of the Crimean War. After another political crisis, more French than English in character, Lord Palmerston became for the first time Prime Minister "to get on with the war." The Peelites, led by Gladstone and without Aberdeen, consented to serve in the Ministry. But they did not serve long ; for Palmerston consented to the appointment of the Roebuck Committee to sit in judgment on his late colleagues, a step Gladstone thought indecent and unprecedented. But there was more behind it than this. He was by now sick of the war, and not convinced that Palmerston would stop it as quickly as possible.

Hence his resignation led to his becoming associated with Bright, Cobden, and the School of Manchester Pacifists, and to his attracting to himself a good deal of the odium that already attached to them. He now attained the maximum of isolation and parliamentary opprobrium. His band of Peelites could still dominate the House under favourable circumstances. His powers as a debater made everyone afraid of him. But there can be no doubt that he was one of the most unpopular figures in Parliament. For who can love a destructive and angular Jesuit?

For the moment, however, Palmerston trimmed his sails to the wind of jingo clamour, and could afford to neglect Gladstone. The Crimean War fizzled out as obscurely and as irrationally as it had begun; the moment it was over England was plunged into the Mutiny, and from the Mutiny into a preposterous claim on China which recalled the Pacifico affair. The Peelites promptly joined a Coalition of Tories, Radicals, and Dissentient Whigs, and Palmerston was again defeated. This time, however, he was to have no nonsense, and, on appealing to the country, had a magnificent triumph in a khaki election. Bright, Cobden, and the Manchester School nearly all lost their seats, and Gladstone was lucky to keep his own at Oxford. Palmerston seemed absolutely safe, when he suddenly fell on the Conspiracy to Murder Bill, a measure to stop England's being made a centre for conspiracies to assassinate

Napoleon III. Gladstone had again defeated Palmerston, and Derby was for the second time called to form a minority Government.

Derby might certainly have formed a fairly stable Ministry could he have had the assistance of Gladstone and the Peelites. Gladstone had always ostentatiously separated himself from the Whigs ; he was always at war with Palmerston, always friendly with Derby, and Protection was dead and buried. On the franchise he had hardly spoken. This time there seemed no earthly reason why he should not join the Government, especially as Disraeli again offered to resign the leadership of the House of Commons to Sir James Graham, a statesman for whom Gladstone had the highest admiration. If Gladstone refused to join, Parliamentary government seemed impossible. However, he refused. He seemed to have an absolute passion for self-immolation, a passion which can only be explained by his reverence for the memory of Peel and hatred for the rôle played in his destruction by Disraeli. But other people who did not fully enter into Gladstone's attitude towards forgotten loyalties may be excused their irritation.

The Derby Ministry, which could thus exist only on sufferance, found itself embarrassed in foreign affairs by the War of Italian Liberation and by the eccentric behaviour of Napoleon III. In home matters they thought they might as well destroy themselves by introducing another Reform

Bill. This went the same way as its predecessors, and yet another General Election took place, in which no party could claim a decisive victory. The wretched business seemed likely to begin all over again, though this time the only possible solution was at hand. The Derby Government fell on the address, owing to an unfounded suspicion that it had intended to intervene on behalf of Austria in the Italian crisis. But Gladstone voted in the minority.

Derby resigned ; the Queen again called on Palmerston ; and in a few days the country heard with astonishment that his Chancellor of the Exchequer was to be Gladstone. He characteristically joined the Whigs at the most unlikely moment, and the Parliamentary crisis, which had lasted since 1846, was over.

CHAPTER III

Joins Lord Palmerston's administration and the Liberal Party – the commercial treaty with France – repeal of the paper duties – quarrel with the Lords – Napoleon III, Nice, and Italy – the panic – Gladstone's war on the estimates – triumph of Gladstone – the American Civil War – Lord Russell's administration – defeat of the Reform Bill – Disraeli's Reform Act – Liberal victory of 1868.

FROM now on Mr. Gladstone was to be the leading figure in English politics : he was to be in office with a single short break till 1874, then from 1880 to 1886, and from 1892 till his retirement in 1894. Why did he do now what he might have done ten years before or even never? How did he come to support the administration of Lord Derby one week and join the Palmerston administration the next ? For nothing seemed to have happened to warrant this particular change at this particular moment. On the contrary, he had undertaken his mission to the Ionian Islands under the Derby administration and seemed nearer the Tories than ever. He was aware that some explanation was necessary, and observed at Ormskirk in 1867 : " Conviction in spite of early associations and long-cherished prepossessions – strong conviction and an overpowering sense of the public interests operating for many, many years before full effect was given to it – placed me in the ranks of the Liberal Party." But these fine-sounding phrases, except in a very general sense, mean nothing, nor are they justified by Gladstone's speeches and writings in the late 'fifties. A variety of motives probably actuated him. Above all, we may believe that his continual isolation was becoming intolerable. Was he for ever to waste his vast administrative gifts in a sterile opposition? Palmerston was now seventy-five and could not go on for ever. Perhaps, too, he could now control this ageing man. A situation, which had been growing continually more strained, at last snapped, and the moment of its snapping was largely fortuitous. But the liberation of Italy offered a bridge between himself and Palmerston. Here at last was a topic in foreign policy upon which they could agree, and had long agreed. His earliest correspondence with Palmerston had risen in 1851 over his letters to Lord Aberdeen about the state of Neapolitan prisons, and Palmerston had been extremely cordial. The Italian question no doubt just made the difference, and enabled Gladstone to get on to the right track at last.

But the reasons which held back Gladstone from joining the Liberal Party were also strong, as is proved by a certain discomfort in his relations with it. In many ways he would have been happier as leader of a Tory Party in which Disraeli had no share. For Gladstone, half Tory and half Radical, was, as Harcourt well said, " never either a Whig or a Protestant," which was a disadvantage in a party which consisted of both. Neither Whig nor Liberal was ever really at home with Gladstone. The Tories would in some ways have been more congenial. For they were more modest in their attitude towards themselves, and were resigned to taking leaders outside their own class. Neither Canning, Peel, nor the more exotic Disraeli were, in the opinion of the " gentlemen of England," exactly out of the top drawer. But, though they might grumble, they were willing to accept the inevitable without serious complaint. It was far different with the Whigs, those happy, hearty high-brows, who regarded the whole world as a cricket-field, with themselves batting and bowling at each end. Why should they call in this renegade son of a Liverpool shipowner, with his preposterous ideas about the Church, to become Captain of the Eleven? It was a monstrous offence against nature.

" I remember your snubbing Theresa Lewis," wrote the delightful gossiping Emily Eden to Lord Clarendon in 1860, " when she said she did not think Mr. Gladstone pleasant, and now you may snub me. I daresay he *is* very clever and he is good-natured, doing his best to bring his mind down to the level of mine, but fails. He is always above me, and then he does not converse, he harangues, and the more he says the more I don't understand. Then there is something about high-church people that I can't define, but I feel it when I am with them – something Jesuitical – but they never let themselves go – and to complete my list of things, there is some degree of Parvenuism about him, as there was about Sir Robert Peel, something in his tone of voice and his way of coming into the room, that is not aristocratic. In short, he is not frivolous enough for me. If he were soaked in boiling water and rinsed till he was twisted into a rope, I do not suppose a drop of fun would ooze out. But I have said all this in the strictest confidence. I go back to the point, that I have been wonderfully fortunate to have such good neighbours, they have given my Broadstairs quite a different tone." [1]

Lord Clarendon may have snubbed his vivacious correspondent, but he must have had a measure of sympathy with her, as we find him writing to Lady Salisbury in 1868 from Rome :

> " Italian art, archæology and literature are G.'s sole occupation. Every morning at 8 he lectures his wife and daughters upon Dante, and requires them to parse and give the root of every word. He runs about all day to shops, galleries and persons, and only last night told me that he hadn't time for the reading room and hadn't seen an English newspaper for three or four days."

But Gladstone never read the newspaper if he could help it, and it is only fair to add that he was to find Clarendon the most " easy " of all his colleagues.

And with the Liberals the situation was not much better. Gladstone might be willing to liberate the Dissenters, but he could not sit at meat with them, talk their language, or share their passions. His mind was always going back to the Oxford Movement, to Leopardi, to Butler, to Dante, to Lucretius, to Homer, things for which Dissenters did not care. He might, in time, have destroyed every church in Christendom, but a churchman he would have remained to the end, preferring the society of Bishop Wilberforce to that of Mr. Binney. Mr. Gladstone trying to be matey over the breakfast-table with

[1] Maxwell, *Life of Clarendon*, Vol. II., p. 224.

a party of tame Dissenting ministers was one of the most painful spectacles to be observed in the London of the 'eighties. The "forest of firm, serious, unintelligent faces uplifted towards Mr. Spurgeon"[1] shared none of his enthusiasms. Thus, when the final crisis came, he quarrelled both with the Whigs and the Nonconformists, and could rely on nothing but his personal prestige. Truly it is a disadvantage to have "not a drop of English blood in one's veins"; and in such circumstances, as Disraeli discovered, it is better to be a Tory.

However, Gladstone found himself in Palmerston's last administration. The Government had a very insecure hold on the House of Commons, and existed on a tacit agreement between Palmerston and Derby that no serious measure of reform would be introduced. Russell, indeed, did produce yet another Reform Bill, but even he hardly pretended to regret its demise. All eyes were turned on the Italian struggle. The only achievements of the Government in home affairs were Gladstone's Budgets and the commercial treaty with France, which certainly saved a grave crisis between the two countries, coinciding as it did with Napoleon's occupation, after a due plebiscite, of Savoy and Nice.[2]

[1] M. Arnold, *Irish Essays*, p. 38.

[2] "The first two years of the new Whig Cabinet saw a terrible danger draw near and recede – war with France. It was averted by Gladstone, Cobden, and Bright *in sweat and agony.*" – Trevelyan, *Life of Bright*, p. 283.

Though England had encouraged the Emperor to join in the Austro-Italian War without taking any risk in the matter herself, the quite reasonable compensation to which Napoleon felt himself entitled in exchange for 50,000 casualties and £30,000,000 expended at Solferino and Magenta lashed the middle classes into a fury. A fine panic prevailed. Now that the Emperor controlled Nice, England no longer controlled the Channel; and unfortunately the crisis about Nice coincided with a crisis in artillery and the coming of the ironclad. So a first-class naval scare was added to a general panic. Irritation grew to madness on both sides of the Channel, and Palmerston, who had been the Emperor's great sponsor, now used language about him which would have been extravagant if applied to his uncle. A huge increase in shipbuilding, combined with a vast scheme for extremely expensive and perfectly useless forts, seemed the proper answer to a non-existent menace; for we now know that Napoleon III, that most unstable of men, was, throughout his whole reign, consistent in one thing only, his belief in the necessity of a good understanding with England. The commercial treaty with France, which at first sailed out amid universal blessings, rapidly lost its popularity. The removal of the paper duties, unpopular with moderate opinion, became still more unpopular when it occasioned a constitutional crisis with the Lords. Gladstone's unceasing warfare with the armament estimates further caused much dissatisfaction. For these reasons he became as offensive in office as he had been in opposition. And the fragility of his position had one very important consequence. It threw him again into the arms of the Radical group, the only section of the House to agree with him about the panic. It is surprising that Palmerston did not seize one of the several occasions Gladstone offered to be quit of him. But he had not a very strong hold on the majority ; he could rely on Gladstone, on several occasions, to turn on the big guns ; he was immensely good-natured, growing very old, and probably did not want more trouble than he could help. In the end the younger man won, though after using methods which will strike many people as peculiar. For he definitely appealed for the assistance of the country to aid him in his tussle with an extravagant and bellicose chief. On the whole, Palmerston was very long-suffering.

" I read with much interest," he writes, " as I came up by the Railway, your able and eloquent speeches at Manchester. . . . I cannot but regret that you should by speeches in and out of Parliament invite an agitation to force the Government of which you are a member to retrace steps taken upon full deliberation and in fulfilment of duties, for the faithful performance of which it is responsible to the crown and the nation. When fourteen or fifteen men are brought together to deliberate on a course of action, it is hardly possible to take exactly the same view of the matter discussed, but some decision or other must be come to, and those who have yielded their own opinions, even when they have not been convinced, do not, when the decision of the body is acted upon, proclaim to the world their dissent from the course pursued"[1]; and a few days afterwards he was able to enclose a leaflet which was very much to the point:

TAXPAYERS
READ
MR. COBDEN'S
NEW PAMPHLET, THE
"THREE PANICS,"
AND JUDGE FOR YOURSELVES

HOW LONG will you suffer yourself to be humbugged by PALMERSTONIANISM, and robbed by the "SERVICES" and others interested in a War expenditure even in times of Peace?

A portion of our Press evidently finds its PROFIT in artificial excitement and WARLIKE SENSATIONS, not scrupling to resort to MISREPRESENTATIONS and SUPPRESSION of the TRUTH in order to further its ends.

THE CHANCELLOR of the EXCHEQUER
APPEALS TO YOU
to help him.

You have the power in your own hands if you will only exert it.

REFORM
THE HOUSE OF COMMONS
and do it thoroughly this time.

[1] Guedalla, *Palmerston and Gladstone*, pp. 205–209.

Palmerston's attitude was absolutely correct. Had he taken advantage of Gladstone's frank offers to resign, he would have been fully justified, and Gladstone could hardly have survived this final shock. But the " cautious hand " refrained, and the explanation must partly lie in a sort of prestige that Gladstone, despite everything, possessed. Morley quotes an anonymous onlooker during this period as saying, " He is the best abused and best hated man in the House : nevertheless the House is honestly proud of him, and even the country feels a glow of pride in exhibiting to the diplomatic gallery such a transcendent mouthpiece of a nation of shopkeepers. The audacious shrewdness of Lancashire married to the polished grace of Oxford is a felicitous union of the strength and culture of Liberal and Conservative England."

Again Palmerston must have been aware of another thing. Gladstone had been trying his hand as a mob orator in several progresses through the north of England, and the Prime Minister had to reckon with his power as an individual. Gladstone had played the highest stakes and won. However questionable from a constitutional point of view had been some of his methods, the Chancellor of the Exchequer could, when the Palmerston administration came to an end with the death of the Prime Minister, look back with some satisfaction on his success.

" When 1866 came, he had managed . . . to

carry expenditure back to the level of 1857. Naval expenditure rose till 1861, and then began to fall: army expenditure rose until 1863, and then began to fall. In 1859, when he went to the Exchequer, the total under these two heads was nearly £26,000,000. When he quitted office in 1866 the total was £24,000,000. In the middle years it had swelled to twenty-eight." Further, Gladstone might boast that by forcing the commercial treaty through the House with the maximum of *brutalité*, he had very likely avoided a war with France. In his six years' warfare *ce terrible Milord* had come off second best, and Gladstone held by 1866 the eventual succession of the leadership.

But though Gladstone had been driven by his quarrel with the House of Lords over the paper duties, and by his hatred of Palmerstonian extravagance, from the extreme right to the extreme left of the administration, he was, even in the course of this development, to accumulate difficulties in his own way. The civil war between the Northern and the Southern States of America threw England into every sort of confusion, political, social, and economic. The cutting off of the cotton supply by the Northern blockade, which was of doubtful legitimacy in the view of international lawyers, reduced Lancashire to great distress, while whether the war was about slavery or not is still a matter that can be argued as endlessly as can the part played by the neutrality of Belgium in 1914. As the hideous struggle continued, bringing increasing misery to England and without the probability of the North ever asserting its superiority, the clamour to intervene in the struggle along with France and Russia grew ever more insistent. The " upper classes " were in favour of America splitting up, while the middle class Radicals and working men were " Northerners." What exactly constituted " correct neutrality " was a problem of great difficulty. On the whole it may be said that the attitude of the British Government was " correct," and Lord Russell (as Lord John had now become) was, in effect, less " Southern " than might have been expected ; even Palmerston, in spite of what Gladstone afterwards said, never really expressed any very strong Southern sympathies in public. Gladstone at any rate never desired to " split up the Union," the continuance of which he thought essential, if we were to retain the loyalty of Canada. On the other hand, the son of the Liverpool slave-owner had to a considerable extent emotional sympathies with the " Sir Charles Burrells, the Sir William Joliffes, the Sir Charles Knightleys, and the Sir Edward Kerrisons " of Virginia, rather than with the bustling industrials of the North. This emotional sympathy with the Conservative South, combined with a firm belief that it must eventually be able to assert its independence, led him into a course of action of which he wrote in 1896 :

"I have yet to record an undoubted error, the most singular and palpable, I may add the least excusable of them all, especially since it was committed so late as the year 1862, when I had outlived half a century. My offence indeed was not only inexcusable, but one of incredible grossness."[1]

During a tour through the north of England, on October 7th, at Newcastle, he uttered the terrible words:

"We know quite well that the people of the Northern States have not yet drunk of the cup – they are still trying to hold it far from their lips – which all the rest of the world see they nevertheless must drink of. We may have our own opinions about slavery: we may be for or against the South: but there is no doubt that Jefferson Davis, and other leaders of the South, have made an army: they are making, it appears, a navy; and they have made what is more than either – they have made a Nation."

Thus Gladstone, at a moment when he had the extreme left in his pocket, proceeded to enrage it. For his speech was an appeal for intervention on behalf of the American counterpart to the landed gentry. He always asserted that this speech was meant to be a friendly act by America, an attempt to stop a bloody and useless quarrel. And for this point of view a good deal may be said. Nearly everyone agreed with Gladstone that the South must win, though they did not quite realise to what extent their own behaviour might be responsible for such a result; or as Henry Adams wrote: "No one knew as well as

[1] Palpable and gross were favourite "strong" words with Mr. Gladstone, e.g. "His error was palpable and even gross" (on Lord Derby's failure to form a Ministry in 1855).

he [Gladstone] that he and his own officials and friends at Liverpool were alone making a rebel navy, and that Jefferson Davis had next to nothing to do with it."[1] Still, for the belief that the South would win, England cannot be too severely blamed. The happy English of those days knew nothing about strategy ; they had indulged in no war since 1815 except in the Crimea, and that war taught no strategy. Thus they could not see how sterile Lee's great tactical victories were. Eventually it was the " Southern " Palmerston who prevented intervention, and he probably knew more about map-reading than any of his colleagues. Few thought the North could win except Bright and his friends ; and their conviction was bred of social prejudice, not of a cooler military judgment. They really preferred the homely North, for they were culturally " Liberal " in a sense that Gladstone never was ; and the differences that were always to reign between Gladstone and his new associates are clearly visible in this differing attitude to the American War. Of the justice of the problem it is now useless to argue. But from one point of view Liberal opinion should have been " Southern." If it was in the order of things that Italy should withdraw from Austria, why should not the Southern States be allowed to withdraw from the Union ? Was Centralisation or Federalism the more liberal form of government ? Were Liberty and

[1] *Education of Henry Adams*, p. 157.

Independence the same thing? Such problems teased Lord Acton, teased Lord Russell, and teased Gladstone. But nothing ever teased the real true-blue Manchester man. For him a prejudice was always a principle; and so Bright was able to support the North without a twinge.

Had Gladstone succeeded in forcing the Cabinet into intervention on behalf of the Southern States, it is difficult to see how he could ever have become leader of the Radical Party. As it was, he lost for the moment all his prestige with it. He was fortunate in being saved from disaster by his backward and reprobate old chief. But as the likelihood of British intervention got more and more remote, as everyone except Gladstone came round to the opinion that the North would win, he was forgiven by his new friends. After all, no eggs had been broken, and his services remained as desirable as ever. Hence his "Conservative" attitude over the American Civil War remains an isolated incident in his career, interesting to the student of his character, but without effect upon his fortunes. And, "strange to say," adds Gladstone in the memorandum already quoted, "*post hoc*, though not *propter hoc*, the United States have been that country in the world in which the most signal marks of honour have been paid me, and in which my name has been the most popular, the only parallels being Italy, Greece, and the Balkan Peninsula."

The 1859 administration drew towards its end,

with Gladstone growing more and more out of hand, as something became suddenly obvious, which few people could have foreseen in 1859. Lord Palmerston was now eighty, Lord Russell well over seventy. Gladstone was the heir presumptive of the Liberal leadership. On two occasions he asserted himself, speaking as a private member from the Treasury Bench, and in a way which much angered his chief. First he asserted in 1863 that he could no longer support in principle the Established Church in Ireland: and secondly he, who had up till then been most lukewarm about reform, suddenly observed during a quite academic debate, which no one thought had any particular significance:

"I call upon the adversary to show cause, and I venture to say that every man who is not presumably incapacitated by some consideration of personal fitness or of political danger is morally entitled to come within the pale of the constitution." Before the astonishment that these words created, he hastily uttered the inevitable qualification, "Of course, in giving utterance to such a proposition, I do not recede from the protest I have previously made against sudden or violent or excessive or intoxicating change." But for once the qualification came too late. Gladstone had trapped himself into saying that he believed ultimately not in this Bill or that Bill or the other Bill, but in household suffrage or in manhood suffrage or in universal suffrage or in any suffrage you like. No doubt he replied correctly, when questioned and harassed on this statement, that his remarks, especially as qualified, had no very definite meaning. But other people equally correctly deduced that they meant a very great deal in the long run. It showed which way the wind was blowing, and the consequences were immediate. His speech on Irish Disestablishment gave him the support of the Dissenters ; that on the franchise, of the trade union leaders. Gladstone's position had undergone a complete change.

Anyone who wishes to make out a case against Gladstone should fix on 1865, rather than on 1885 for their study. For this was the only time when he embarked on a change of policy which redounded to his immediate advantage. On the question of the Irish Establishment he can easily be defended, and has defended himself in "A Fragment of Autobiography," an essay as candid and modest as anything possibly could be. The relationship of Church and State was the most constant interest of his life, and he was entitled to develop in any way he wished. To question him on this point is an impertinence. His attitude on the suffrage is in different case. For he had never interested himself deeply in the matter, and his sudden enthusiasm is suspicious. As his early career shows that he possessed an absolute genius for avoiding power and his later life an equal genius for losing it, we may acquit him of gross tergiversation. He was often masterly in tactics but reckless and improvident in strategy, and nobody who has studied him carefully will say that he took up the suffrage cynically to obtain power. But we may argue more subtly that the Gladstone of 1865 felt quite a different person to the Gladstone of 1859. It was in the 'sixties that he first left the House of Commons and went into the country. Up till then, as member for Newark and for Oxford, he had not even had to address a constituency. He sat in the House, alien in mind to most of those who surrounded him and spinning his theories to himself, the most isolated figure in politics. In the 'sixties all this was changed. He began to perceive that the greatest of all his gifts, that of a platform speaker, had, up till that moment, rusted in him unused. The discovery of this enormous power must have been immensely exciting to him, and a conclusion followed on the heels of the discovery. If he had such a way with electors, it stood to reason that electors should be more numerous. Also he had learnt from John Bright what could be achieved upon the hustings. And Gladstone, though he was always scraping his conscience, was not very self-conscious in the modern manner. His whole being kindled with the warm atmosphere he created when he came for the first time in direct contact with his fellow men. When the election of 1865 came, he finally lost his seat for Oxford, as a result of his speech on the Irish Church, and was plunged into a short sharp campaign in South Lancashire.

A few lines in his diary seem to sum up the whole change in his life and spirit.

"*July* 16*th*, '65. Always in straits, the Bible in church supplies my needs. To-day it was in the first lesson, Jer. i. 19. 'And they shall fight against thee, but they shall not prevail against thee, for I am with thee, saith the Lord, to deliver thee.'

"*July* 17*th*. Again came consolation to me in the Psalms lxxxvi. 16. It did the same for me April, 1853. At night arrived the telegram announcing my defeat at Oxford as virtually accomplished. A dear dream is dispelled. God's will be done.

"*July* 18*th*. Went off at eleven . . . to the Free Trade Hall, which was said to have 6,000 people. They were in unbounded enthusiasm. I spoke for an hour and a quarter and when the meeting concluded went off to Liverpool. . . . Another meeting of 5,000 at the Amphitheatre if possible more enthusiastic than that at Manchester."

It was at the Free Trade Hall in Manchester that he uttered the famous phrase, of such immense psychological significance: "At last my friends, I am come among you, and I am come among you unmuzzled."[1]

"I congratulate you," wrote Palmerston, who did not misunderstand the significance of Mr. Gladstone's campaign, "on your success in Manchester, though many friends would have preferred seeing you still for Oxford."

A more reflective character than either, the Bishop of Saint David's wrote to a friend about

[1] "It is true, I believe, that, on the day of his rejection (for Oxford), the Bible fell out of the hand of the statue of James I on the gate tower of the Bodleian, an omen of the separation of the Church from the State. The stone being very friable, the fall was not miraculous, although it was curiously apt."—Goldwin Smith, *My Memory of Gladstone*, p. 27.

the same time from Abergwili Palace, "He [Mill] is evidently, like Gladstone – in whom for a time it was as little suspected – a man of vehemently passionate susceptibility. The snow covers a volcano."[1] But in Gladstone's case the snow had permanently melted under the sun of a Northern constituency and the volcano was to erupt with increasing violence till the end.

In the election of 1865 the cheerful octogenarian regained his mandate from the constituencies. The Liberals were to remain in office, as long as they attempted nothing Liberal. Palmerston himself seemed in perfect trim, and all was for the best in the best of all possible worlds.

"I do not see any reason," he wrote to Gladstone on October 7th, "for calling the Cabinet together till November." On October 18th, the inevitable and the impossible occurred. Lord Palmerston died, and Lord Russell reigned in his stead. Lord Russell was now seventy-three years old. Thirty-three years before, he had passed the Great Reform Bill through the House of Commons. And for the last fifteen years he had been endeavouring to round off this great achievement with a further effort on a smaller scale. When withdrawing his Bill in 1854, on the outbreak of the Crimean War, he had wept over the table with disappointment. On the verge of the grave, he was once more given an opportunity, and Gladstone, now leader of the House, introduced

[1] *Thirlwall Letters*, p. 171.

a Bill of studious mildness, which might just have a chance of going through. It was reckoned that some 400,000 people including about 150,000 working men, would get the vote.

Chances of success were, however, remote. The Liberals indeed had a comfortable majority. But the House was essentially Palmerstonian and hostile to reform. The right wing Liberals entered into an opposition as furious as it was trifling.

> " The Rt. Hon. Gentleman [Mr. Horsman]," said Bright, " is the first of a new party, who has expressed his great grief, who has retired into what may be called his political cave of Adullam and has called about him everyone that was in distress and everyone that was discontented. The Rt. Hon. Gentleman has been anxious to form a party in this House. There is hardly anyone on this side of the House who is able to address the House with effect, whom he has not tried to bring over to his party or Cabal and at last the Rt. Hon. Gentleman has succeeded in hooking the Rt. Hon. Gentleman the member for Calne [Robert Lowe]. . . . When a party is formed of two men so amiable – so discreet – as the two Rt. Hon. Gentlemen, we may hope to see for the first time in Parliament a party perfectly harmonious and distinguished by mutual and unbroken trust. But there is one difficulty which it is impossible to remove. The party of two reminds me of the scotch terrier, which was so covered with hair, that you could not tell which was the head and which was the tail of it."

There can, however, be no doubt which was the head and which the tail of it. Lowe, one of those men " who make discord wherever they appear," in a succession of diatribes which remain as amusing as any speeches delivered in Parliament, dominated the House for a session and destroyed the Bill. It passed the first reading, indeed, by a majority of five, to be subsequently defeated in Committee. The triumph was Lowe's, and many of his prognostications have since been justified by the event, though they had no relation to the Bill. But neither had Gladstone's speeches in defence of his own measure. This trifling proposal was simply the occasion for an outburst of rhetoric on the advantages and disadvantages of pure democracy. The defeat in Committee was not necessarily fatal. But the Government, seeing that victory was hopeless, after some hesitancy resigned, and Russell retired from active politics. He was a shocking old Whig. But it is impossible to deny him a measure of sympathy.

Hence for the third time Disraeli became leader of the House in a minority Government, pledged like its predecessor to some sort of Reform. The old game seemed likely to be played out again. But as Gladstone had got bored in 1859, so, now, Disraeli got bored in 1866. Within a few months some two million working men had been added to the register, and Disraeli had proved to his own satisfaction that he at any rate had been perfectly consistent throughout. Even Gladstone was "awed by the diabolical cleverness of Disraeli," who, in a general way, allowed Gladstone to amend the measure as he would. The Bill, which had been introduced as a parliamentary fraud, emerged as Household Suffrage, of which nobody had even dreamed a few months before. Enthusiasm outside was terrific; for the trade unions, which since the collapse of Chartism had neglected politics, had at last returned to an interest in the franchise, and Gladstone, with some justice, got the credit for Disraeli's Bill. Thus he suddenly became the leader of two million working-men electors; and quickly showed that he was not the man to let the grass grow under his feet. An immediate General Election was impossible, owing to the inevitable delay in compiling the new register. But in a few weeks he had tabulated his resolutions for the disestablishment and disendowment of the Irish Church. His proposals excited to the utmost pitch the enthusiasm of his supporters, while the Tories, themselves split on the subject, were unable to offer an effective opposition. This was perhaps Gladstone's most brilliant achievement as a leader. Both the strategy and the tactics are beyond criticism. Disraeli might think that he had "dished the Whigs." He had indeed been dazzlingly brilliant. But he was soon to find that he had dished no one but himself. By firmly attacking the franchise difficulty, he had done no more than pull a rotting tooth out of the festering jaw of the Liberal Party. The new skin closed quickly over the healthy cavity. Whig and Radical, Adullamite and Manhood Suffragist, united at last behind a leader and a policy, rushed with a howl into the fray.

CHAPTER IV

Gladstone Prime Minister – Irish Disestablishment and the Irish question – the Education Act – the opening of the Civil Service and University reform – the Franco-Prussian War – arbitration with America – achievements and unpopularity of the Government – defeat of the Irish University Bill – General Election – defeat of the Government – Disraeli Prime Minister.

" I am by no means sure," wrote Gladstone in his autobiographical notes, " that Providence has endowed me with anything that can be called a striking gift. But if there be such a thing entrusted to me, it has been shown at certain political junctures in what may be termed appreciation of the general situation and its result. To make good the idea this must not be considered as the simple acceptance of public opinion founded upon the discernment that it has risen to a certain height. It is an insight into the facts of political eras and their relation to one another, which generates in the public mind a conviction that the materials exist for the formation of a public opinion and for directing it to a particular end."

IN 1863, Gladstone, while supporting in theory the destruction of the Irish Church, said that the matter was not within the scope of actual politics. In 1868 he came to the conclusion that " a public opinion " could be formed and a General Election fought upon the subject. In this he was doubtless assisted by the enfranchisement of large numbers of Nonconformists. But he was assisted by other circumstances. In 1867 the Fenian plots spilt over from Ireland into England. In September at Manchester a body of armed men rescued two Fenian prisoners from a police van and accidentally shot a policeman, for which three men were hanged. In December a Fenian rolled a barrel of gunpowder up to the wall of Clerkenwell prison, where a comrade was confined, and fired it. The explosion blew down part of the wall and killed several people. Out of this unpromising material, Gladstone "formed a public opinion" and gained a majority of 100; for few people had taken much interest in the Irish Establishment till Gladstone had drawn their attention to the subject.

Gladstone had evidently an extremely subtle and even tortuous mind, yet he often blurted out the most unpalatable truths at the most unnecessary moment. We have seen him doing this over the income tax in 1854. He did the same, to the annoyance of many people, over the Fenian outrages.

> "In my opinion, and in the opinion of many with whom I communicated, the Fenian conspiracy has had an important influence with respect to Irish policy. . . . The influence of Fenianism was this – that when the Habeas Corpus Act was suspended, when all the consequent proceedings occurred, when the tranquillity of the great city of Manchester was disturbed . . . then it was when these phenomena came home to the popular mind and produced that attitude of attention and preparedness on the part of the whole population of the country which qualified them to embrace . . . the vast importance of the Irish controversy."

Similarly in 1880, Gladstone admitted frankly that the criminal activities of the Land League proved that his Land Act of 1870 had been inadequate and must be expanded. Again in 1885, after the first election in which the Irish democracy had voted, the resultant triumph of Parnellism showed that Ireland wished for Home Rule, and that arguments to the contrary, drawn from turbulence and outrage, were either irrelevant to the issue or strengthened the Home Rule position. Such frank speech, galling to the pride of the audiences he was addressing, is a proof of intellectual candour, infinitely refreshing in politics, which are too often conducted in a world of humbug.

From the point of view both of Gladstone and England the election of 1868 has its peculiar importance, for it was at this moment that Gladstone decided to tackle the Irish problem and to devote some thirty years to its attempted solution. In 1868 we are presented with the first fruits of this decision, the Disestablishment of the Irish Church, the Land Bill of 1870, and the unsuccessful Bill of 1873 to set up a Catholic University. This was called the attempt to "cut down the three branches of the Upas Tree," that is to say, the Protestant ascendancy in Religion, Land, and Education. In 1880 Gladstone perceived that he had been unsuccessful; and the result was the Irish Land Act of 1881. In 1886, after another General Election, the programme was still perceived to be incomplete. The result was the Home Rule Bill of 1886. But here the "Old man in a hurry" tried, unlike himself, to rush the country, split his party in the effort, ruined his own activity, and was reduced to the state of solitude described by Cardinal Manning. It is useless now to discuss either whether Gladstone's Home Rule Bill could have saved the Irish Connexion, or even whether the Connexion was worth saving. Probably nothing short of a republic could ultimately satisfy Ireland. But we can study the tireless devotion of Gladstone to an idea, a devotion which led to his becoming Prime Minister at eighty-three, and for all his prestige, one of the most solitary men in England. His official life may be split into two halves; from 1841–1863, when he was the architect of Free Trade, and from 1868–1893 when he endeavoured to solve the Irish problem. In the first he was successful. In the second he failed, but he has gathered round his name all the beauty which is attached to failure.

The administration formed by Gladstone in 1868 was the most efficient instrument of government to hold office in England between the Cabinet of Sir Robert Peel in 1841, and that of Sir Henry Campbell-Bannerman in 1905. Gladstone's purely personal activities were confined to the three first-class Irish measures mentioned above. The Ministry, however, passed a mass of legislation, most of which, in an ideal state, would have been voted before the Enfranchisement Bill of 1867. There were few vested interests on which the Government did not lay a sacrilegious hand. The first measure was quite properly the disestablishment and disendowment of the Irish Church on which the election had been won. This passed through the House of Commons triumphantly, to be amended out of all substance in the House of Lords. On the amendments Gladstone refused to yield, in spite of immense pressure from the Court, the House of Lords, the Church, and a body of his own supporters. Gladstone, when occasion arose, was always willing to negotiate. But he also knew when to stand firm, and he stood firm now though the last thing he could have wished was a quarrel with the Lords. His instinct was justified. At the last moment the Lords collapsed, and he then threw them a little money to save their faces. He had gambled and won. In 1870, he passed the great Education Act, which made education universal. With the drafting of this measure he had little to do personally, but, by allowing public money to swell the funds of Church schools, he quarrelled with a large section of his Nonconformist supporters, who, with great ingratitude, abstained, in considerable numbers, from voting in 1874. The Ballot Act was passed after it had once been rejected by the House of Lords. College and University offices were thrown open to Nonconformists at Oxford and Cambridge, and open competition, without prior nomination, was introduced into all branches of the Civil Service, except the Foreign Office.

Purchase of army commissions was abolished by Royal Warrant after a Bill to that effect had been obstructed in the Commons and rejected by the Lords. The Home Secretary, Bruce, passed a Mines Act, which, though emasculated in committee, " forms the basis of modern mining legislation."[1] A Licensing Bill was passed through the Commons by the same Minister, giving new powers to magistrates to limit the number of public-houses, and also shortening hours for the sale of drink. This Bill was thrown out by the House of Lords, and was reintroduced and passed, with the section devoted to limiting the number of public-houses omitted.[2] An important Local Government Bill was withdrawn and Stansfeld's measure, though loyally supported by Disraeli, was but a shadow of the Government's intentions.

In foreign politics the Government was equally successful. By getting a promise from both France and Germany to respect the neutrality of Belgium, England kept out of the Franco-Prussian War. By accepting the principle of arbitration for damage done to American vessels by British ships sailing under Confederate colours during the American Civil War, we succeeded in healing a constant quarrel with the United States. The sum paid, about £3,000,000,

[1] Cole, *Short History of the Working Class Movement*, Vol. II., p. 72.

[2] Even this milder measure was so unpopular that its repeal by the Disraeli administration was expected. Cross, however, did no more than amend it slightly.

may have been excessive. But, as the United States originally asked for sums estimated variously at £400,000,000 and £1,600,000,000, we did not do so badly, and, by entrusting a question of national honour to an international court, we set an example to the world, which the world has been not very willing to follow. Nor can the Government be justly blamed for failing to prevent Russia taking advantages of the Franco-Prussian War to repudiate the Black Sea clauses of the Peace of Paris of 1856.

At home, trade continued good, taxes were reduced, and surpluses were as regular as they were substantial.

"Except in the matter of the Education Act," says Bagehot, "the Government made no mistakes." Yet by 1872 it was one of the most unpopular administrations that England has experienced. Everybody was offended, nobody satisfied, and the party was at sixes and sevens. Disraeli, in a speech at Manchester, put in perfect language what everybody had been thinking:

"Extravagance is being substituted for energy by the Government. The unnatural stimulus is subsiding. Their paroxysms end in prostration. Some take refuge in melancholy, and their eminent chief alternates beneath a menace and a sigh. As I sit opposite the Treasury Bench, the Ministry reminds me of one of those marine landscapes, not very unusual on the coasts of South America. You behold a row of exhausted volcanoes. Not a flame flickers on a single pallid crest. But the situation is still dangerous. There are occasional earthquakes, and ever and anon the roaring of the sea."

We can see how the Education Act had annoyed the Nonconformists, and the University Bills had annoyed the Church. On the other hand the Irish were not in the least grateful for the assaults on the Upas Tree. The abolition of Purchase irritated what army men were still Liberal. The Mines Acts were distasteful to the coal-owning Liberals and to the supporters of *laissez faire* generally. The Licensing Act inconvenienced not only that important mass of Her Majesty's subjects, which was seized with a sudden thirst at three o'clock in the morning, but also the trade union leaders, who, it appeared, always did their business after midnight in public-houses. The newly enfranchised working classes had better claims to a grievance, for, though nearly the whole legislative output of 1868–1874 has eventually worked to their advantage, they got very little immediate return for their money. The unions, profiting from a trade boom, were growing, like strikes, in power and numbers, and Gladstone, having given them one Trade Union Act at the beginning of his administration, refused to give them another. The surpluses, which merely went to reduce income tax, failed to stimulate enthusiasm in a class of voter which would not pay income tax anyhow. The admirable foreign policy of the Government appeared pusillanimous and boring. Administrative scandals loomed vast. The Chancellor of the Exchequer, Lowe, introduced a tax on matches with a joke, "*ex luce lucellum*" (a little tax on light). In face of the popular outcry the tax was withdrawn. There were also irregularities in the Post Office. The First Commissioner of Works insulted Dr. Hooker of Kew Gardens, and Science was mobilised against the Government. A peace policy carried with it large reductions in the dockyards, which further reinforced the opposition, though, in truth, most of the economies had been sketched out by the preceding administration. The Prime Minister's own seat at Greenwich was in danger. We must remember, too, that this was the first Government to be harassed seriously by the by-election nuisance.

Finally, when Gladstone introduced his Irish University Bill, to set up a Catholic University in Ireland (an admittedly truncated measure), he was met by a monstrous coalition of Tories, Nonconformists, Catholics, and Atheists. The Bill was defeated on the second reading and Gladstone resigned. But on Disraeli refusing to take office, he resumed it for a few months, passing the Judicature Acts in a final paroxysm.

The Prime Minister had thus to face the country, with his party thoroughly disorganised and without a programme of any kind. The election finally came in an absurd manner. Gladstone temporarily added the Chancellorship of the Exchequer to his other office, and many lawyers stated that he had thus forfeited his seat for Greenwich, which, it was generally thought, he was bound to lose. This legal squabble precipitated the election, which was fought on the abolition of the income tax.

This "cry" has been cited by Mr. Buckle[1] as a proof of Gladstonian unscrupulousness. I cannot assent to this view. His conduct was "slim," but not unscrupulous. Certainly he could not get through the Cabinet before the election, the reductions in the Army and Navy Estimates necessary for the abolition of the tax. But had he won the election, his regained prestige would have enabled him to have his way.[2] This is what Gladstone called "doing things in the right order." However, there was no earthly chance of winning the election. By 1874 the "People's William" had sunk woefully in popular estimation.

[1] Buckle, *Life of Disraeli*, Vol. V., p. 274.

[2] The slump which began in 1874 would have prevented him. But this was not evident in 1873 and Gladstone was consistent in his policy. – See Clapham, *Free Trade and Steel*, p. 404.

CHAPTER V

Resignation of Gladstone – his abstention from politics never complete – the Bulgarian Atrocities – re-emergence of Gladstone – the Treaty of Berlin – Disraeli's Expansionist policy – Egypt – Transvaal – Afghanistan – Zululand – the Midlothian Campaign – fall of the Beaconsfield administration.

THE General Election of 1874 returned Disraeli to effective power when he was too old and ill to give England the full advantage of his talents. Gladstone recognising, as he had to do, the complete reversal of his fortunes announced his resignation from the leadership and his own retirement from active politics. No one had, he affirmed, ever been an effective Prime Minister after sixty, while he had so many interests, literary, scholarly, and ecclesiastical, that he would not find the time heavy on his hands. Wise onlookers applauded his decision.

"This is the real explanation," wrote Bagehot in the *Economist*, "of Mr. Gladstone's resignation. He can withdraw into comparative retirement, because he can be absorbingly occupied in retirement. . . . That Mr. Gladstone has judged wisely for himself in resigning the leadership of the Liberal Party we cannot doubt. There can be little pleasure in leading that party in its present state, and there must be much vexation. . . . The toil of attending Parliament merely 'to watch the proceedings'; to sit opposite to a Government in the anxious hope that it may make some mistake, and with little to say if it does not; to detect errors in figures and poke amendments into clauses – is an excellent training for young members, but a dismal employment for a finished statesman."

This is true enough. But it was a somewhat Arcadian picture of a great statesman conscious of services rendered, who is only too anxious to retire into private life, to

> train his quincunx and to draw his vines.

Life at Hawarden must have been far less agreeable for the family. For Gladstone was extremely angry both with the party and the country. We can imagine that more than once "his face hardened and whitened, the eyes burned as I have seen them once or twice in the House of Commons when he was angered – burned with a deep fire." In the summer of 1874 the Emperor of Russia paid a visit to England, and a luncheon was given at Marlborough House. Disraeli, as Prime Minister, sat in the place of honour. Gladstone was less prominently seated. "When the company rose after luncheon, Disraeli turned to his rival and said, in allusion to the latter's absence from Parliament, with a mixture of comedy and tragedy expressed on his countenance, 'You *must* come back to us : indeed we cannot possibly do without you.' Gladstone with more than usual severity answered, 'There are things possible and things impossible: what you ask me is one of the things that are impossible.' Upon this, Disraeli turned to me [Stanley] as the nearest representative of the public present, and said, 'You see what it is – the wrath, the inexorable wrath of Achilles.' "[1]

It is in the nature of Achilles to issue from his tent. But while the hot fit is on, there is no *arrière pensée* in the retirement. And Gladstone

[1] *Life of Stanley*, Vol. II., p. 447.

had more than one intellectual Briseis to while away his ennui, particularly the Infallibility of the Pope. For he took the promulgation seriously, and his pamphlet *The Vatican Decrees*, in which he argued that the doctrine of Infallibility broke the cord of civil obedience, only showed how profoundly the most intelligent and well-informed observer can misconceive the prudent policy of Rome. Thus in theological and classical controversy, with his large family around him, in the Temple of Peace, or, axe in hand, amid the ash-trees in the park, Gladstone intended to devote to spiritual preparation the few years which still separated him from the grave. As his life and strength were to be so abnormally prolonged, this retirement could in any case have hardly been permanent. A French duchess asked Fouché during his period of service under Louis XVIII, how he could in early youth have perpetrated the Massacres of Lyon. "You see, Madame," he answered, "one must have one's finger in the pie." Gladstone, too, could hardly have kept his fingers out of the pie. But his absences from Parliament might have become more frequent, had he not, against all expectations, kept his seat for Greenwich ; and had not Disraeli, to please the Queen, passed through the House the Bill "to put down ritualism." This gratuitous attempt to tamper with the consciences of clergymen in order to please the Lutheran in Windsor, was the one thing calculated to bring Gladstone up from

Hawarden to London, and prevent abstention from debate becoming a habit. Otherwise there seemed little reason for his interference. The early record of the new Government was beyond cavil. Cross was, if possible, an even better Home Secretary than Bruce. Excellent measures passed one after the other through the House. After a short tussle with the Radical Group, the leadership of the Liberal Party passed into the safe hands of Lord Hartington : and no political squall appeared on the horizon. Till 1876 there was no sign that the Government of the peaceable Disraeli would divagate into the excesses of imperialism, before subsiding into the quicksands of a trade-slump. There is no point in emerging from one's tent to find an armistice in full operation all along the windy plains of Troy.

But the occasion for the battle was near at hand. The truce was over. The warfare was to become more bloody than ever.

In May 1876 an abortive rising by Bulgaria led to the Bashi Bazouk suppression known as the "Bulgarian Atrocities," dismissed by Disraeli in the House of Commons as "coffee-house babble." Excitement spread all over the Balkan Peninsula. The result was the despatch to Turkey of what is known as the "Andrassy Note," signed by Germany, Austria, and Russia. To this note England, France, and Italy conformed. After the murder of the French and German Consuls at Salonika, the "Andrassy Note" was followed by the " Berlin Memorandum," to which Disraeli, on a point of punctilio, refused to subscribe. This refusal precipitated the campaign of Gladstone, as it offended him on his two deepest susceptibilities. First of all, because Disraeli came forward by this action as the supporter of the Turk against the Christian in the Peninsula ; secondly, and perhaps even more important, because, by an act of insensate folly, England broke up " the Concert of Europe," on which Gladstone, with some vision of a League of Nations ever before his eyes, had always insisted as the basis for any respectable polity. By this last action, too, Disraeli was implicated in all the humiliations which followed. Russian volunteers poured into the Balkans for the war against Turkey, and marched to the gates of Constantinople, without England daring to intervene by force of arms. Disraeli's own cabinet was split, the resignation of Lord Derby being a most serious loss. Lord Salisbury was then left to make the best of a very bad business. If Russia did not take Constantinople, the thanks were due not to the British Government but to Bismarck. By the Treaty of Berlin, four-fifths of the Russo-Balkan terms were granted, and the English were bought off with Cyprus, which was absurdly thought to be useful as a base for the defence of Turkey in Asia. The Government's Eastern policy was as wounding to the national vanity as it was politically indefensible, and it is impossible to believe that Disraeli was in full possession of his faculties when he embarked on such a course. His correspondence was never more amusing than at this moment. But what with the gout, his Elizabethan flirtation with Queen Victoria, and his senile passion for Lady Bradford, he seems to have lost much of his grip on public affairs.

The Eastern question brought Gladstone out of retirement. But his anger was further excited by the whole foreign policy of the Government, which became progressively tainted with imperialism. The Ministry seemed seized with a frenzy of expansion, illustrated by granting the title of Empress of India to the Queen ; by the purchase of the Suez Canal shares, which brought as a corollary the " Dual Control " in Egypt ; by the high-handed annexation of the Transvaal ; by Lord Lytton's forward policy in Afghanistan, leading to the disastrous Afghan War ; and by Bartle Frere's obsession with the Zulus which led to the catastrophe of Isandlwanah and the final destruction of the Zulu power. In fact, by the time Gladstone got back to office in 1880, the stage was set for the great British expansion, about which, most certainly, it is possible to have two opinions.

The Whigs, in the House of Commons, had not protested with much energy against Disraeli's Balkan policy. But there can be no doubt that it was unpopular with many branches of the community. The Prime Minister's light-hearted attitude to the Bulgarian massacres outraged both the High Churchmen and the Nonconformists, and thus rendered possible the reforming of the Liberal Party and the "creation of a public opinion." But Gladstone had in no way contributed to the excitement save by the publication of *Bulgarian Horrors* in September 1876, and the immense sale of this pamphlet was rather a proof of the excitement already created. In his diary we see that he is amazed at the violence of public opinion, aroused without his ever being on the stump.[1] For the first few months, indeed, Gladstone was busy "catching up." We may admit that he caught up very quickly, and brought off his third successful attempt to "create a public opinion." By the time the Treaty of Berlin was signed in 1878, he may be said to have won on the main issue, for the Disraeli Cabinet was divided and the treaty recognised most of what Gladstone had striven for. But a larger issue loomed ahead – the whole question of imperialism, the raising of which entailed a further consequence extremely damaging to Gladstone's subsequent efficiency as Prime Minister – his quarrel with the Court.

Gladstone having got the Cabinet on the run, did not give it time for breath. At the age of seventy his vitality was as great as ever, and, by the force of his personality and by his excellent strategical position, he was able single-handed to restore for the moment the unity of the party.

[1] Lord Gladstone, *After Thirty Years*, pp. 129–131.

The Whigs were induced to follow the lead of Gladstone in his Balkan campaigns, while the Radicals, owing to their dislike of imperialism, were willing for a space to forget the Home Policy, in which they differed from Gladstone himself and still more from the right wing of the party. Thus Gladstone not only directed public opinion, but recreated the instrument which could put that public opinion to effective use. At the beginning of 1876, the Liberal Party was almost non-existent ; by the end of 1877, it was united, enthusiastic, and self confident. " The old man " had indeed performed a miraculous task, of which the coping-stone was the Midlothian campaign.

Towards the end of 1879 it was suggested that Gladstone, who was already chosen as Liberal candidate for Leeds, should fight the County of Midlothian in the Liberal interest. The constituency was mainly agricultural, and, as the agricultural voter at present hardly existed, the electorate numbered in all but some four thousand persons. On the other hand, it was situated at the very gates of Edinburgh. It was dominated by the Duke of Buccleuch, and the sitting member was his eldest son, Lord Dalkeith. Thus Gladstone was fighting not only against the vested interests of the Buccleuch family, but he was fighting for Edinburgh, for Scotland, and, as it turned out, for the whole of Great Britain. The " Pilgrimage of Passion " enraged the whole of " Society " at the moment, and has since become the symbol of an irresponsible and emotional demagogy. It is treated all through Mr. Buckle's Life of Disraeli as a monstrous amalgam of lies and tosh. This was the view adopted at the moment by Disraeli, Society, and the Queen. "It is certainly a relief," Disraeli wrote to Cranbrook, "that this drenching rhetoric has at length ceased, but I have never read a word of it. *Satis eloquentiae, sapientiae parum.*" At an earlier date he had already announced his whole attitude to the Gladstonian resurrection. Gladstone had, quite correctly as it turned out, called the Cyprus Convention "an insane covenant." "But," Disraeli replied, "I would put this issue to an English jury. Which do you believe most likely to enter an insane convention, a body of English gentlemen honoured by the favour of their sovereign and the confidence of their fellow subjects, managing your affairs for five years, I hope with prudence and not altogether without success, or a sophistical rhetorician inebriated with the exuberance of his own verbosity and gifted with an egotistical imagination that can at all times command an interminable and inconsistent series of arguments to malign an opponent and glorify himself?" The picture is to be sure a very witty one. But it contains all the fallacies dear to the parliamentary speaker. First of all Disraeli attributed to the "gentlemen of England" his own exotic romanticism, which had, as a matter of fact, exasperated most of his aristocratic colleagues. Secondly, the ordinary jury represented by the electorate decided at the earliest possible opportunity that Disraeli had governed their affairs neither with success nor prudence ; and thirdly, the personalities were introduced by Disraeli himself. His own imagination was as egotistical as anyone's.

" Gladstone's style gives me a headache," wrote Disraeli more than once. And as Disraeli was one of the best letter writers that have ever lived, his opinion has gone down on the Midlothian campaign. The effect of turning to these speeches after reading the abuse of them, is overwhelming. Far from being demagogic, they are often pedantic, and chock full of references to international law and European history. There was never any great attempt to prove that the Government had sacrificed, in any immediate sense, the interests of the country. The appeal is entirely to the moral order, to the iniquity of imperialism and excessive power. The *pede poena claudo* is the only bogey which he holds up. Never again does the speaker suggest any immediate advantage as likely to accrue from voting for him. He gives no pledge. He can suggest no material reason why the electors of Midlothian should give him their vote. He indeed gives every reason why they should not, and a reading of the Midlothian speeches, which is in itself a liberal education, fills one with disgust for the squalors of modern electioneering. Gladstone succeeded in uniting the country around a moral issue – the hatred of imperialism. You may well disagree with him on the points at issue. You may say that he was aided, beyond his own imagining, by the unprecedented trade depression. But the Midlothian campaign must be about the only successful example of leading a party to victory by an appeal to nothing but moral standards.

Mr. Buckle, with great skill, chooses for quotation the most violent passages in the Midlothian campaign :

"At home the Ministers have neglected legislation : aggravated the public distress by continual shocks to confidence, which is the life of enterprise : augmented the public expenditure and taxation for purposes not merely unnecessary but mischievous ; and plunged the finances which were handed over to them in a state of singular prosperity, into a series of deficits unexampled in modern times. . . . Abroad they have strained, if they have not endangered, the prerogative by gross misuse : have weakened the Empire by needless wars and unprofitable extensions : and have dishonoured it in the eyes of Europe by filching the Island of Cyprus from the Porte, under a treaty clandestinely concluded in violation of the Treaty of Paris. They have aggrandised Russia : lured Turkey on to dismemberment if not her ruin ; replaced the Christian population of Macedonia under a degrading yoke and loaded India with the costs and dangers of an unjustifiable war. From day to day, under a Ministry called, as if in mockery, Conservative, the nation is perplexed with fear of change."

Gladstone's style disgusts Mr. Buckle so much, that he does not stop to consider one thing. We are asked to "rub our eyes and marvel how even self-righteousness and jealousy could so pervert the doings and aims of Ministers." He barely stops, however, in his disgust for the style, to argue whether or not this ill-composed indictment be true. While if it comes to humbug, which contains the most – this perfectly clear analysis of the late Government's policy (with which half Disraeli's colleagues agreed), or Disraeli's own election address?

> "Rarely in this country has there been an occasion more critical. The power of England and the peace of Europe will largely depend on the verdict of the Country. Her Majesty's Ministers have hitherto been enabled to secure that peace so necessary to the welfare of two civilised communities and so peculiarly the interest of their own. But this ineffable blessing cannot be obtained by the passive principle of non-interference. Peace rests on the presence, not to say the ascendancy, of England in the councils of Europe. Even at this moment the doubt supposed to be inseparable from popular election, if it does not diminish, certainly arrests her influence, and is a main reason for not delaying an appeal to the national voice. Whatever may be its consequences to Her Majesty's present advisers may it return to Westminster a Parliament not unworthy of the Power of England, and resolved to maintain it!"

"The national voice" had no doubt, when consulted, as to where the rights of the matter lay. But then it did not suffer, like Disraeli and Mr. Buckle, from an excessive tendency to sick headache.

Excitement ran high all through the election, unfortunately high for the calm government of a nation. When you appeal successfully to a country on a purely moral issue, the defeated opposition will naturally be factious. In Edinburgh and around, the population went mad with enthusiasm. When at last it was announced that "the Grand Old Man" had carried the safe Tory seat against the man who owned the whole county, the northern metropolis was seized with a delirium, of which *The Times* newspaper gives a lively description :

"The Liberals are in ecstasies. But the more sober-minded are mingling thanksgiving with their mirth. They never hid from themselves the risks Mr. Gladstone was made to run by his being brought down here at his time of life, and at so momentous a political crisis, to contest a peculiarly constituted constituency. . . . The constituency numbers only 3,620 and the number polled was 2,947, or fully 90 per cent.[1] This is quite as large as had been anticipated. When the result was announced, it was received with deafening cheers and the wildest yells. The news spread like wild-fire through the city. To-night the streets are thronged by excited crowds, whose feelings again and again find vent in loud cheers for Gladstone. . . . Preparations had been made outside Lord Rosebery's town residence in George Street where a crowd of several thousands was soon assembled. . . . The broad and handsome street was lighted up with lime lights. Mr. Gladstone, having been called for, stepped on to the balcony and addressed a few words of thanks to the vast multitude. His reception was enthusiastic beyond all description and when he withdrew the cheers were again and again renewed. In response to loud calls Lord Rosebery then came forward and spoke a few words of congratulation. The scene was an extraordinary one, one that Mr. Gladstone is not likely to forget. After repeated cheers for the member for Midlothian, Mrs. Gladstone and for Lord Rosebery, the crowd moved to the front of the Conservative Club in the same street, and indulged in a counter-demonstration. The *Scotsman* office in Cockburn Street

[1] The figures were : Gladstone . . 1,579
Dalkeith . . 1,368
Majority 211

was the next point made for. There also vigorous cheers were forthcoming, the youths evidently believing that noise was conducive to good workmanship. The crowds have continued to perambulate the principal streets of the city during the whole evening. The excitement in Edinburgh is positively wild. What the feeling in Dalkeith Palace may be it is not difficult to imagine. The reverse in Midlothian coming so soon after the repulse in Dumfriesshire is undoubtedly a crushing blow to the Buccleuch influence. By these two elections, the fate of 'faggotting' has probably been sealed."[1]

And all this pother because an old gentleman of seventy, who was not even the leader of a political party, had been stumping round the suburbs of Edinburgh, expatiating on the theme that you ought to think of other people beside yourself.

But the enthusiasm in Edinburgh was at least equalled by the disgust and astonishment of Mayfair and Windsor. The Queen and Disraeli, who had been breathing in an exquisite ether of toadyism and exaltation, learned with incredulity, then with despair, that they were to tread no longer the silken path of dalliance. True, they had both cut themselves off from all contact with reality. But the Liberals, too, were amazed by the size of the majority. The by-elections had been good, but none too good. A stalemate, a majority of ten or twelve, would have satisfied the Barrington Erles of the Reform Club. But Gladstone, by his Midlothian speeches, had dragged the country after him, and he found himself, even more than the Liberal Party, returned with a majority of a hundred.

[1] *The Times*, April 5th, 1880.

CHAPTER VI

Gladstone again Prime Minister – hostility of the Court – the Whigs and the Radicals in the Cabinet – withdrawal from Afghanistan – bombardment of Alexandria – Majuba – Khartoum – the Bradlaugh affair – the Land League, Coercion, and the Land Act – the Kilmainham Treaty – murder of Lord Frederick Cavendish – the Pendjeh affair – the Third Reform Act.

FOR some little time the Queen had decided that she could never again send for Gladstone. "I could never take Mr. Gladstone as my Minister again," she had written to Lady Ely in September, ". . . for I never COULD have the slightest *particle* of confidence in Mr. Gladstone *after* his violent, mischievous, and dangerous conduct of the last three years." At first sight, it looked as if the "Fairy" might be spared the crowning humiliation. For Gladstone was not nominally the leader of the Liberal Party, and the Queen acted correctly in sending first for Lord Hartington and Lord Granville the leaders in the Commons and the Lords. But these had no intention whatever of pulling chestnuts out of the fire for Queen Victoria. The victory had been Gladstone's, not theirs, and the country wanted the Old Man. Nor indeed would it have been possible to form a majority without him. No one knew the proportion of "Whigs" to "Radicals" in the new House, and Gladstone was the only person who could keep the party together for a few years more. So, on April 23rd, 1880, the unwelcome form of Gladstone was once more ushered into the Royal Closet.

We cannot know to what extent he had been prepared for the welcome he was to expect, for there was nothing in his official past to warrant the Royal anger. As early as 1868, indeed, that first-class gossip, Lord Clarendon, had given a hint of unpleasantness. "I hope the Missus," he wrote to Lady Salisbury, "will send for the Pembroke Lodger [Lord Russell] because it would please him and assuage his pain at getting older as time goes on : but for her own interest she ought to send for the elect of the people and to give no colour to the notion that is rife of his being utterly repugnant to her." The Queen did send for the "elect of the people," and her relations with him were, if occasionally formal, correct. She did not like Ayrton, who was intolerable to everyone, and she was suspicious about Childers and Cardwell. But Cardwell was a prig and Royalty is always fussy about the services. Still even the use of the Royal Warrant to abolish Purchase, though inconvenient to her owing to the hostility to the measure of her cousin, the Duke of Cambridge, who was commander-in-chief, did not meet with improper opposition. She merely insisted on a special memorandum being drawn up, so that the exceptional circumstances could be made clear and put on record. It was the Disraelian flattery of 1874–1880 which had gone to her head, exacerbated her temperament, and rendered her angry and sulky with everyone else. The failure of the 1880 administration can be largely attributed to the time wasted quarrelling with the Court.

At the very starting-point the unfortunate Prime Minister, who two months before had been receiving the frenzied devotion of a whole people, found himself between two fires. First he seems to have had no conception of the Radical strength in the new party. He was surprised to learn that it would be necessary to give Chamberlain office, and still more that Dilke and Chamberlain hung together. Eventually Dilke was satisfied with an under-secretaryship. But while attacked for lukewarmness by Radicals at home, he was attacked for contrary reasons at Court. On April 27th the Queen had expressed regret at seeing among the names of those submitted to her "such very advanced Radicals as Mr. Chamberlain and Sir Charles Dilke." Next day she notes in her journal, "Another letter from Mr. Gladstone submitting more unexpected names! Mr. Mundella, one of the most violent Radicals for President of the Board of Agriculture [not in the Cabinet], the equally violent, blind Mr. Fawcett as Postmaster-General [not in the Cabinet]." However, the Government was somehow formed, and the long-drawn-out battle between Queen and Prime Minister began.

The situation was bound to be trying, for Gladstone returned to power morally engaged to "clear out everywhere." The ideal policy, from his point of view, would have been to clear out of Afghanistan, to clear out of the Transvaal, and to clear out of Egypt. But such a scheme was obviously impossible, quite apart from the fury it would arouse at Court. Hence temporising inevitably began. Gladstone successfully cleared out of Afghanistan straight off. Over the Transvaal he wavered, hoping that the information from South Africa, that the Boers were yielding, would turn out to be true. Majuba was the result of this temporising, but Gladstone, to his eternal honour, and to the rage of Court and Society, refused to avenge this defeat; so we got out of the Transvaal, though with heavy damage. In Egypt he was even less successful. A military rising against the existing Government led to British intervention at Alexandria, desertion by France (the other partner in the dual control), the resignation of Bright, and further responsibilities in Egypt. The despatch of Gordon, with instructions to "evacuate the Sudan," led to the ghastly muddle which ended at Khartoum, and it looked as if we would have to add the Sudan to our Egyptian responsibilities. Here, again, he stood firm and refused to "avenge Gordon," an achievement which drove the Queen to a white heat of indignation, and, indeed, infuriated most of the middle classes. So Gladstone failed heavily in his attempt to undo the Expansionist policy of the Disraeli Cabinet, and, at the same time, made himself detested as a cowardly Little Englander, who had sat down under the insults of Majuba and Khartoum. Certainly affairs were badly mismanaged. The Colonial Office misled him over the Transvaal situation, though as Prime Minister he must take the blame for this. It is difficult to see, however, how he could have behaved otherwise than as he did about Egypt. He did extract himself from Afghanistan, and, though in the most unfortunate manner, kept out of the Sudan. Gladstone certainly consented to the appointment of Gordon ; but it is, I think, fair to say that had he not been partially incapacitated by influenza at the critical moment, Gordon would never have started for Khartoum, or, even if he had, the instructions he received would not have been so obscure. But with the Court, half the party, and all the opposition, bent on a policy of expansion, it is difficult to see how Gladstone could have fulfilled the hopes with which he took up office.

The home situation, too, was as miserable as that abroad. Before the first session was a week old, the Bradlaugh affair was in full blast. The opposition, as factious as it was angry, saw that the Liberal Party could, as always, be split in two over a question of religious liberty, and the Prime Minister rapidly found himself in a minority. The Irish Land League, which the Disraeli administration had allowed to grow up unchecked, now burst with full force on its successor, and the Government embarked on the traditional, the useless, the inevitable policy of suppressing the Land League by coercion, while granting large measures of redress in the form of a new Land Bill. It is easy to find fault with this system, which perhaps does no more than take all grace out of concession. But it is difficult to see how a Government can sit by quite inactive, and watch a growing campaign of outrage and murder. It can be further argued that the Land Bill was perfectly useless in itself; that strengthening the position of the tenant *vis-à-vis* the landlord, the abolition of excessive rent by special rent courts, the recognition of free sale, etc., was the wrong way of approaching the subject; and that the real solution was Land Purchase. This had long been the view of Bright, who was now powerfully reinforced by Matthew Arnold. On the other hand the Radical Group of the Liberal Party strongly objected to the plan of buying off bad landlords; and the Conservative Party, too, when it finally passed Land Purchase, was surprised to find that it in turn had failed to solve the Irish problem. From a purely personal point of view, however, the passing of the Irish Land Act of 1881 is one of Gladstone's supreme achievements. The subject was squalid, the details arid and tiresome beyond imagination. Few people were interested in the subject, still fewer knew anything about it. The Irish Party, enraged by Coercion Acts and the incarceration of their colleagues in Kilmainham Gaol, devoted their energy to proving that the Bill was absolutely useless. Yet the prophet of Midlothian never lost his patience, never lost his mastery of detail, nor his control over the House, and, after a committee stage of unparalleled exhaustion, the third reading was passed almost without opposition. No subject could well be more dead than that of Irish Land. But anyone who wishes to know why Gladstone held his unique parliamentary position might do worse than study the debates (particularly in committee) on the Land Bill. Rarely can a man of seventy have got through such a heavy and distasteful piece of work with so little thanks from anybody, and while agonising problems, spreading from the Transvaal to Afghanistan, were occupying the attention of Parliament during all the remaining intervals for business. The 1880 Ministry was certainly a failure, but the spectacle of Gladstone, harassed between his quarrels with the Court and dissension among the two groups in his Cabinet, turning from Bradlaugh to Kruger, from Egypt to Ireland, from Montenegro to Berlin, conscious at the back of his own mind that he could no longer assent, intellectually, to the Union, fills one with a Plutarchian belief in the possibility of greatness. He was a Grand Old Man.

Sir Pomeroy Colley was killed at Majuba, Gordon was butchered in Khartoum, but Gladstone was to suffer nearer home. By the

"Kilmainham Treaty," Parnell and his colleagues were liberated from prison, the Coercion Acts were to be allowed to lapse, and a new attempt was to be made to grapple with the Irish problem. The chief secretary resigned and his place was taken by the Prime Minister's nephew, Lord Frederick Cavendish, a man of immense personal charm, whose close relationship with the Prime Minister was to be a symbol of the new policy. On his arrival in Ireland he was murdered in the Phœnix Park, and all hopes of a better understanding ended. Even Parnell realised that for the moment nothing could be done, and indeed he thought of retiring from politics altogether. Chamberlain, moreover, was much disappointed that Cavendish and not himself had been sent to Ireland, and the result was a widening of the rift between the Prime Minister and his dangerous young colleague. It is difficult to conceive a more tragic situation, and one that contrasted more lamentably with the great Government record of 1868.

Gladstone might well have been crushed by this succession of disasters, public and domestic. Yet such was the great spirit of the man, that he seemed to rise invigorated from defeat. His firm intention not to "avenge Gordon" and add responsibilities in the Sudan to responsibilities in Egypt, to wash out blood in more blood, to avenge massacre by massacre, was rendered possible by Russian aggression in Afghanistan, culminating in what is known as the "Pendjeh affair." To the astonishment of the Russian Court, £11,000,000 were voted for War Estimates and the Egyptian army was hurried off to India. This was a marvellous success ; for by the time the Russian Government had given way, the army was thousands of miles from Khartoum ; and no one seriously suggested that it should go back again.

But the "Old Parliamentary Hand" had other cards up his sleeve, and, amid general astonishment, it was announced that the agricultural labourer was to receive the vote before the next election. For the full triumph of this masterstroke Gladstone was indebted to the folly of the Tories. Had they supported the Bill heartily, there is no reason to suppose that the agricultural vote would have gone predominantly Liberal. But by a generally disobliging attitude, by repeating the old quarrel about enfranchisement and redistribution, and by nearly precipitating a constitutional crisis, the opposition succeeded in presenting the new electorate to Gladstone, with the results that we shall see. It would have been difficult to have played a thoroughly bad hand more consummately. But the Enfranchisement Bill of 1884 is so intimately associated with the Home Rule split that we shall do well to start afresh from this point.

CHAPTER VII

The Reform Act and Home Rule – "The Caretakers' Administration" – the General Election of 1885 – its unsatisfactory result – Gladstone declares for Home Rule – the Liberal split – the General Election of 1886 – defeat of the Liberal Party – the Parnell affair – the General Election of 1892 – the Second Home Rule Bill – its defeat by the Lords – Gladstone on the House of Lords and the Navy Estimates – resignation of Gladstone – illness – death – estimate of his failures and achievements.

On June 8th, 1885, the Government was unexpectedly defeated on the Budget, over a proposal to increase the beer and spirit duties, and Gladstone resigned. As in 1868, however, it was impossible to have recourse to an immediate dissolution owing to the new register being incomplete. The Queen, therefore, sent for Lord Salisbury, who formed "The Caretakers' Administration."

But for some months before this defeat the Cabinet had been in a state of division amounting to dissolution. The Crimes Act was to expire in August, and what was to succeed it? Gladstone and Chamberlain had put before the Cabinet a scheme for a "Central Board" allowing large measures of local government to Ireland. This scheme was supported by all the Commoners in the Cabinet except Lord Hartington, and opposed by all the Peers except Lord Granville. Thus the "Home Rule Split" was already in full operation; only, which is all-important, Chamberlain was on the same side as Gladstone.

Parnell was incidentally so anxious for the "Central Board" that, could he have got it, he would not have opposed a moderate Crimes Act. The bright young people of the Conservative Party, led by Lord Randolph Churchill, however, saw a fine opportunity, and announced that they had no intention whatever of supporting a further Crimes Bill, and led Parnell to believe that they would give him almost anything. The defeat of the Government on the Budget was the first result of the alliance between the Conservative opposition and the Irish Nationalists. Lord Salisbury, therefore, came into office pledged to an "Irish" policy. The relations of the Salisbury Government with Parnell can be read with very conflicting accounts in a dozen biographies[1]: and fortunately the biographer of Gladstone is excused from discussing them. As, however, his behaviour over Home Rule has been so severely blamed, it is well to bear in mind that "The Caretakers' Administration" enjoyed until the election the support of Parnell, and that the Conservatives received the Irish vote at the General Election of 1885.

At the moment of the General Election the situation was as follows. The Liberal administration had split upon a Central Board. The Conservative minority Cabinet had unofficially "gone one better," thereby completely changing

[1] It is impossible not to deplore the absence of candour with which the distinguished biographer of Lord Salisbury has treated these important months in her father's life.

the situation, as Parnell would no longer take what would have satisfied him before. The General Election then occurred with all parties in a state of flux. The result was disastrous. Without the Irish vote, Gladstone could not form a stable administration ; Lord Salisbury could not do so even with it. Hence the Irish vote was no longer of any use to the Conservatives.

On this result becoming apparent, Gladstone, without consulting his party, entered into direct negotiations with Lord Salisbury, through the medium of Mr. Balfour and made a definite offer. If the Conservatives would " settle " the Irish question, he would support them. As we know, the offer was refused. But the incident shows the complete independence of Gladstone towards his own party and towards the country. He now considered that it was his duty to get rid of the Irish problem : and he believed that his position in the country would enable him to do it. Then he could clear out. It was certainly a miserable prospect for a statesman of seventy-five to go on remaining in public life merely to prevent Hartington and Chamberlain quarrelling. The future no doubt rested with Chamberlain. But Chamberlain must really fight his own battles. Gladstone was there to solve the Irish question over the head of party passion, but for no other reason. And he thought, with the self-confidence born of tremendous achievement, that he could, preferably by negotiation, or, if that failed, by public campaign, drag the party after him; that he could once more "create a public opinion."

The negotiations collapsed; the Government fell on Mr. Jesse Collings's motion to give "three acres and a cow" to each agricultural worker; and Gladstone returned to office to solve the Irish question in the place of Lord Salisbury. Parnell was beginning to regret that under his orders the Irish had presented some thirty seats to the Conservative Party.

Gladstone must have now recognised that he had got to get rid of the Whigs. Hartington had "dug his toes in" since 1883. Having crushed the Central Board in 1884, he was not likely to alter his mind in 1886. The Whigs had got to go, and this was a good moment for getting rid of them. It was essential, however, to keep the Radicals, and it was Gladstone's failure to do this which precipitated the catastrophe. The line that separated him from Chamberlain was a thin one, and it is difficult to believe that this alone was responsible for the break. On the other hand, a different explanation is also unsatisfactory. Perhaps Gladstone did not appreciate the strength of Chamberlain, though his diary is full of flattering references to him. On October 8th, 1885, he had written to Granville, "Chamberlain came yesterday and I had a great deal of conversation with him. He is a good man to talk to, not only from his force and clearness, but because he speaks with reflection, does not misapprehend or (I think) suspect or make unnatural difficulties, or endeavour to maintain pedantically the uniformity and consistency of his attitude throughout."[1]

This does not look as if Gladstone thought Chamberlain an *arriviste* or a cad. Nor did Chamberlain ever hide his admiration for Gladstone. " Mr. Gladstone was a bad judge of men and literature [!]," he observed in 1898, " but was so far above other men that he saw no difference between Harcourt, Bright, and Childers. From a high mountain all things look equal."

From a personal point of view, Chamberlain had grounds for annoyance. The Whigs had turned down his Central Board a few years before, and now he was expected to give much more. He saw Lord Spencer, whom he particularly despised, first straining at the gnat and then swallowing the camel. This is always exasperating. Further, it is urged that Gladstone ought to have offered him something much better, say, the Chancellorship of the Exchequer, now that the Whigs had gone. No doubt this is so, though Gladstone cannot be very severely blamed for wishing to avoid the scene that such an appointment would have caused at Windsor. Besides, it could hardly matter to Chamberlain what office he was given ;

[1] I have, since writing this, read an advance copy of Mr. Garvin's *Life of Chamberlain*. The personal estrangement is revealed in stronger colours. But the book does not enhance one's respect for Chamberlain's political imagination.

a man of his ability can make his own office, and with Hartington out of the way, he had the leadership in his pocket, as soon as Gladstone went. We may perhaps be content with saying that he saw the Home Rule campaign would collapse, and did not wish to sacrifice his radical programme to Irish fantasy. Here, however, he argued absurdly. There is no reason to suppose that the Home Rule campaign would have collapsed without the defection of Chamberlain. As it was, the new Radicalism was heard of no more for twenty years, and when at last it revived, no one attacked it more violently than its inventor.

These obscure negotiations are, however, important, not only because they destroyed Gladstone as an effective force in politics, but because they illustrate both his weakness and his strength. His weakness was a certain clumsiness in personal relations, an inability to have it out properly with his interlocutor, or even with his party. Lord Acton had observed this as early as 1880, and written tactfully to Gladstone's daughter, Mrs. Drew :

"I wonder whether . . . a thing we all perceive remains a mystery to the person most concerned to know it. The Liberal Party is held together, not by forces within, but by a force above it. . . . Without Mr. Gladstone's ascendancy and the lustre of his fame, Harcourt, Argyll and Bright would soon offend every group into insubordination and incohesion. The jealousy between the old Liberals who are losing ground and usurping Radicals, and all other familiar elements of discontent cannot be restrained by

Parliamentary management alone. There remains a great sphere for direct personal influence. The men Mr. Gladstone used to look up to, Peel and Aberdeen, had not much of this and I fancy that he takes from them the belief that it is unnecessary or undignified. He has been so long without holding the threads of party . . . it is so natural to him to underrate the effect of direct personal contact, that he may think that the sole legitimate method of mastering men is Parliamentary speaking or writings addressed to mankind. But it is worth anything that people should know and see more of him, in society if possible. . . . I am sure that all public policy can do to strengthen the government will be done. But I note an unhappy impatience of those inferior arts my earthly spirit relies on."

It was easy perhaps to point to the disease, but it was harder to suggest a remedy. Gladstone did not shine in an atmosphere of tea-table trifles. A colossal and rather starchy highbrow, he had a mind that ran along lines alien to all his colleagues. It is notable that his favourite "pupil," Morley, had an intellect as isolated as his own. Nor was his deficiency remedied by any great social capacity on the part of Mrs. Gladstone, whose vagueness could be as inconvenient as it, in retrospect, is delightful. If some dissenting ministers were asked to breakfast, they were always the wrong dissenting ministers. If a peer were asked to lunch, he was sure to be the wrong peer. Never so much as in 1886 did Gladstone suffer from being "neither a Whig nor a Protestant." It is impossible that Disraeli should have so muffed a crisis.

But whatever may have been the social incompetence of Gladstone in 1886, we cannot but be amazed at the self-confidence with which this old gentleman of seventy-six grappled with a shattering position. Having separated from both the Whigs and the Radicals, he would get on without them. He had quarrelled with the maximum number of politicians, but he would appeal over their heads to the country. He would be in no sense of the word a party man. Gladstone took a long time to reach his opinions, but, having reached them, he understood their implication. It is this which differentiates him from almost all politicians. In 1885 the Irish agricultural labourer, that is to say, the Irish democracy, had voted for the first time. The vote was a crushing, almost unanimous, appeal for Home Rule. The metaphysician in Gladstone could argue from the general to the particular. If the Irish wanted Home Rule, they must have it. Bright thought otherwise. He disliked "Irish rebels"; and therefore thought an exception should be made to the rules. Not so Gladstone. Gladstone could reason. Bright could only make poetry out of a prejudice.

Thus the third administration was formed, for the purpose of introducing a Home Rule Bill. Everything else had now gone by the board. Gladstone had assumed the last of his many rôles. The great legislator was now no more than a flame, the incarnation of an ideal, which men either would or would not worship. His face had assumed that extraordinary whiteness, accentuated by the two black orbs of his eyes, which gave an incandescent light to the Pilgrimage of Passion. This is the evangelist of whom Traill wrote in his *New Lucian* :

"Sir, I can only tell you that profoundly as I mistrusted him, and lightly as on the whole I valued the external qualities of his eloquence, I have never listened to him even for a few moments, without ceasing to marvel at his influence over men. That white-hot face, stern as a covenanter's yet mobile as a comedian's : those restless flashing eyes : that wondrous voice, whose richness its northern burr enriched as the tang of the wood brings out the mellowness of a rare old wine : the masterly cadence of his elocution : the vivid energy of his attitudes : the fine animation of his gestures."[1]

"You will never know Mr. Gladstone's strength," remarked Chamberlain, "till he has parted from all his colleagues."

The only course seemed to go straight ahead. A Cabinet was to be formed, the Bill rushed through the House of Commons, and, if defeated, an appeal would be made over the heads of Parliament to the country. Wiser heads, perhaps, suggested a different procedure. Introduce the Bill, lay it on the Table of the House, and give opinion time to mature. But the "old man in a hurry" could not wait, as before he had shown so incomparably how to wait. Perhaps he suspected, not without reason, that the moment he was gone, Home Rule would be decently

[1] Traill, *The New Lucian*, pp. 305, 306.

buried. Those new men, a Harcourt or a Rosebery, what did they care about his ardours and endurances, his metaphysical frenzy, the divine amenities of an impeccable deduction? He was now over self-confident. Having searched always for authority, he did so still, and found the authority in himself. He would simply *make* the English public vote away the Union. Whigs, Radicals, Dissenters, what were they? He could call them to heel. The British public would follow where he hollooed.

And perhaps it might have done so, had it been left to itself. But it is the great achievement of democracy to accumulate obstacles between the elector and the expression of his opinion. The election was lost before ever it began. For the Conservative Party announced, with consummate skill, that no Liberal who voted against the Home Rule Bill would be opposed at the Election. Ninety-one members with unsafe seats found this bait too sweet to be resisted. They threw out the Bill and came safely back to Parliament. The prophet fell crashing into a trap. Gladstone was lucky indeed not to lose control over the whole Liberal organisation. It was an achievement, perhaps, to turn the Birmingham organisation against its maker, Chamberlain. Still the terrific gambler had had his final throw and lost.

The General Election of 1886 marked the end of Gladstone as a practical force in politics. He had now eaten his way through the whole nineteenth century. Having helped to smash the Tory Party in 1846, he had smashed the Liberal Party, single-handed, forty years later. For thirty years, he had been the biggest figure in England, the most passionately adored, the most bitterly hated. Had he wished, he could have shaken the throne to its foundations, and he had refrained. In his ultimate ideals he had failed. He had not secured self-government for Ireland : he had himself been compelled to add vast tracts to the British Empire. Though still the idol of half England, he was now more solitary than ever, and might as well have abandoned the game.

But this was what Gladstone never could, nor would, do. He had thrown up the leadership of the party in 1874 ; he had wished to do the same in 1884. He knew he was not the man to grapple with the economic problems of the new age. But he would not admit he was beaten. The Union was to be modified : and he was the only man to modify it. Till then, the Liberal Party must put up with its leader whether it wanted him or not, and many were his colleagues, who did not hide their irritation at his undue longevity.

So it was that in 1886 Gladstone did not abandon the leadership of his miserably shrunken party. He was, in fact, to be Prime Minister again for a short time in 1892. Deaf and blind, he was to show that he had lost none of his parliamentary skill. But his majority was but a miserable shadow of what he had hoped. The Liberal reaction, which had first set in as a result of Parnell's exposure of *The Times*' articles, "Parnellism and Crime," and the revelation of Pigott as a forger, received a fatal set-back with the catastrophe of the Parnell divorce case.

To form an opinion of Gladstone's conduct of this extremely trying incident, it is necessary to study the subject with some care. Everybody who does so without bias, will, I think, admit that Gladstone personally emerges with as much credit as such a squalid story permits. The matter must be put in its historical cadre.

Gladstone and Parnell entered on the disastrous election of 1886 in a state of unjustifiable optimism. Parnell knew nothing about England. Gladstone's immense self-confidence led him to believe he could carry the country with him as in 1868 and in 1880. But, being an "old man in a hurry," he did not allow the affair time to ripen. The Chamberlain Party smashed the official leader. But Gladstone continued as Liberal leader, waiting for the tide to turn. The Coercion Bills, which followed the formation of the Conservative Government, began for the first time to test the conscience of the British public, and for this new fact in English politics the Irish campaigns of Mr. Gladstone must be given full credit. The by-elections went favourably for the opposition, and everything seemed in excellent trim for the next appeal to the country. On October 22nd, 1890, a by-election in the Eccles

Division of Lancashire sent Liberal hopes sky-high. This would have but one meaning. The Nonconformists, who had been frightened away in 1886, were returning to the fold. But there was a fly in the ointment ; for, at the end of 1889, the Irish leader had been made a party in a divorce suit, the petition having been filed by his colleague O'Shea. But Parnell never showed by a single tremor that he had any fear about the result. On November 10th, 1890, Morley had a long interview on general matters with Parnell at the Metropole Hotel, Brighton. At the end of the conversation, he said to Parnell : " 'There's one point on which I have no right to speak to you – and if you don't like it you can say so. But it is important that we should know whether certain legal proceedings soon to come on are likely to end in your disappearance from the lead *for a time.*'

" He smiled all over his face, playing with his fork.

" 'My disappearance ! Oh, no. No chance of it. Nothing in the least leading to disappearance, as far as I am concerned, will come out of the legal proceedings. The other side don't know what a broken-kneed horse they are riding.' 'I am delighted to hear that,' said I, 'for I, for my part of course, regard you as vital to the whole business.' 'Well,' he said, 'the Irish people are very slow to give a man their confidence and they are still more slow to withdraw it.' I inferred from his talk of the broken-kneed horse that he meant there would be no adverse decree."[1]

On the 13th, Morley told Gladstone, relying on the above conversation, that "Parnell would emerge as triumphantly from the new charge as he had emerged from the obloquy of the forged letters."[2] The case came on two days later. It was obvious at once that Parnell would lose it. The decree was pronounced on November 17th, and Parliament was to meet on the 25th. Gladstone assumed that Parnell would resign the lead, but was firm that it could have nothing to do with him.

"Many thanks for your letter," he writes to Morley on November 18th . . . "But I think it plain we have nothing to say and nothing to do in the matter." Gladstone's first instinct was to say nothing about it, though the situation must have been exasperating. Unfortunately, again, the *canaille* of the Liberal Party were meeting at Sheffield on November 21st and 22nd, and Morley and Harcourt were to attend in order to interpret to Gladstone, with all their matchless insight, the reactions of the Nonconformist conscience to this most delicate matter.

Gladstone wrote again to Morley on the 19th, "Your appeal as to your meeting of to-morrow gives matter for thought. I feel: (1) That the Irish have abstractedly a right to decide the question;

[1] Morley, *Reminiscences*, Vol. I., pp. 253, 254.
[2] Morley, *Life of Gladstone*, Vol. III., p. 429.

(2) That on account of Parnell's enormous services – he has done for Home Rule something like what Cobden did for Free Trade, set the argument on its legs – they are in a position of immense difficulty ; (3) That we, the Liberal Party as a whole, and especially we its leaders, have for the moment nothing to say to it, that we must be passive, must wait and watch. But I again say to myself, I say I mean in the silent and interior forum ' It'll na dee.' I should not be surprised if there were to be rather painful manifestations in the House on Tuesday. It is yet to be seen what our Nonconformist friends . . . will say."

" Our Nonconformist friends," the usual radical *queue* of well-to-do Quakers and ambitious Wesleyans in the Sheffield pulpit, had no doubt whatever as to what they should say. If Parnell remained head of the Nationalist Party, there must be something rotten in the great Liberal principle of Free Institutions. Candidates began withdrawing ; and it was with the greatest difficulty that the Chairman, Spence Watson, was prevented from delivering a violent philippic against Parnell from the platform. The agnostic Morley and the Erastian Harcourt returned to London in a panic. The Dissenters had spoken ; the new Moloch must be appeased. It was certainly a pity that neither Gladstone, Harcourt, nor Morley were themselves Nonconformists. They might have taken the bluster at its proper value.

So Harcourt and Morley came limping back to London, while Gladstone exasperated everyone by lingering on at Hawarden. He did not arrive in London till Monday, November 24th, where he was met in Lord Rendel's house by Granville, Harcourt, Arnold and John Morley. According to Lord Rendel, Gladstone arrived furious with Parnell, in a panic about Colman the mustard king, and with his mind completely made up. But what happened does not support this, though we may suspect that Gladstone's nerves were pretty badly frayed. On one point he remained firm. He would base no action on any moral judgment. " What," he cried, " because a man is called leader of a party does that constitute him a censor and a judge of faith and morals? I will not accept it. It would make life intolerable." But Morley and Harcourt, crowned with the laurels of Sheffield, would not let the Old Man escape. Without Parnell, he could be Prime Minister in two years' time, and grapple again with the Irish problem. With Parnell, the Liberal Party would plough the sands of opposition for six years more, and even Gladstone could hardly introduce a Home Rule Bill at ninety. In no case need Parnell's feelings be considered, he knew the situation perfectly well, and he had lied shamelessly. Had he cared for Ireland as much as for himself, he would have quietly withdrawn for a space. There was in any case no question of an election for two years, and in two years much can be forgotten. The arguments are good ones and there is no Pecksniffery about them. All this pressure, acting on his own very natural anger and disappointment, induced Gladstone to " write " his letter to Morley. As it seems widely held that the letter was a piece of sanctimonious humbug, it had better, long as it is, be quoted in full :

" My dear Morley,

" Having arrived at a certain conclusion with regard to the continuance at the present moment of Mr. Parnell's leadership of the Irish Party, I have seen Mr. McCarthy on my arrival in town and have enquired from him whether I was likely to receive from Mr. Parnell himself any communication on the subject. Mr. McCarthy replied that he was unable to give me any information on the subject. I mentioned to him that in 1882, after the terrible murder in the Phœnix Park, Mr. Parnell, although totally removed from any idea of responsibility, had spontaneously written to me and offered to take the Chiltern Hundreds, an offer much to his honour, but one which I thought it my duty to decline.

" While clinging to the hope of a communication from Mr. Parnell, to whomsoever addressed, I thought it necessary viewing the arrangements for the commencement of the session to-morrow to acquaint Mr. McCarthy with the conclusion at which after using all the means of observation and reflection within my power I had myself arrived. It was that notwithstanding the splendid services rendered by Mr. Parnell to his country, his continuance at the present moment in the leadership would be productive of consequences disastrous in the highest degree to the cause of Ireland. I think I may be warranted in asking you so far to expand the conclusion I have given above as to add that the continuance I speak of would not only place many hearty and effective friends of the Irish cause in a position of great embarrassment, but would render my retention of the leadership of the Liberal Party almost a nullity. This explanation of my views I begged Mr. McCarthy to treat as confidential and not intended for his colleagues generally, if he found that Mr. Parnell contemplated spontaneous action. But I also begged that he should make known to the Irish Party, at their meeting to-morrow afternoon, that such was my conclusion, if he should find that Mr. Parnell had not in contemplation any step of the nature indicated. I now write to you in case Mr. McCarthy should be unable to communicate with Mr. Parnell as I understand you may possibly have an opening to-morrow through another channel. Should you have such an opening I beg you to make known to Mr. Parnell the conclusion itself, which I have stated in the earlier part of this letter. I have thought it best to put it in terms simple and direct, much as I should have desired, had it lain in my power, to alleviate the painful nature of the situation. As respects the manner of conveying what my public duty has made it an obligation to say, I rely entirely on your good feeling, tact, and judgment."

It is perhaps a pity that this letter was ever written. Two observations, however, may be made on it. It was evidently intended to be private ; it avoids any moral censure and merely says, in effect, " You can get Home Rule out of me, and not out of anybody else. If Parnell stays, we shall be out of office, not for two years more but for eight ; and I can't introduce a Home Rule Bill at ninety. Draw your own conclusions."

But, if we now turn from Morley's *Life* to his *Reminiscences*, it looks as if the old man tried to wriggle out of the mess at the last minute, as if indeed he had hardly composed the letter independently.

" At 8 to dinner in Stratton Street. I sat next to Granville, and next to him was Mr. G. We were all gay enough and as unlike as possible to a marooned crew. Towards the end of the feast Mr. G. handed to me at the back of Granville's chair the draft of the famous letter in an unsealed envelope. While he read the Queen's speech to the rest, I perused and reperused the letter : Granville also read it : I said to Mr. G. across Granville 'But you have not put in the very thing that would be most likely of all things to move him.' Harcourt again regretted that it was addressed to me and not to P. and agreed with me that it ought to be strengthened as I had indicated, if it was really meant to effect P.'s mind. Mr. G. rose, went to the writing-table and *with me standing by* wrote on a sheet of Arnold M.'s grey paper the important insertion. I marked then and there under his eyes the point at which the insertion was to be made and put the whole into my pocket. Nobody else besides H. was consulted about it or saw it. After the letter came to be printed, Mr. G. remarked to me that he thought the insertion was to be a postscript. He did not complain or care, but was it not so? 'No,' I said. 'It really was not : I marked the place in pencil at the moment.' Just imagine ! P.S. By the way I forgot to mention that if he does not go, my leadership of the Liberal Party is reduced to a nullity. What a postscript to be sure !

"Walked home by midnight, with pretty serious thoughts for the morrow. Glad to find my head cooler than most."

A strong impression remains : (1) That Mr. G. tried to wriggle out of the thing till the last minute ; (2) That at the end of a very long and trying day, at eighty-one he was hardly clear as to what he was doing ; (3) That Harcourt and Morley wrote most of the letter.

Next day, when the Irish Party re-met to elect their leader, Parnell elaborately kept out of the way, well knowing that mischief was afoot, and McCarthy failed to communicate Gladstone's letter to the meeting, without or with Parnell's permission, a failure of duty which can probably be ascribed to personal cowardice. The result was that the Nationalist Party re-elected Parnell leader.

Then the Liberal leaders, in ignorance of McCarthy's defection, were jauntily informed by the Irish leader that he had just been re-elected. The consternation was, as may be imagined, considerable, and Gladstone (and this was his great mistake) favoured the immediate publication of his letter, a step about which Morley seems to have hesitated. With its publication, the collapse of Parnell and the division in the Nationalist Party followed inevitably. It was also a mistake from the point of view of Gladstone. For a letter which was intended as an appeal was published as an excommunication.

At the end of the year Gladstone was again discussing the Irish question with Morley, and observed: "You have no regrets at the course we took?" J. M.: "None, it was inevitable. I never doubted. That does not prevent bitter lamentation that inevitable it was." Gladstone evidently had his regrets.

That the whole business was lamentably muddled, no one will deny, and probably the catastrophe would have been avoided had not the divorce proceedings, the Liberal gathering at Sheffield, and the meeting of Parliament, all followed within the course of a week. From the biographical point of view, we would say that all through, save during the inevitably obscure colloquy on the Front Opposition Bench, which ended in the publication of the letter, Gladstone had had his hand forced. Mr. Ervine in his able life of Parnell expresses amazement that Gladstone submitted to the "impertinence" of Stead, the Rev. Hugh Price Hughes, Spence Watson, and others.[1] This is not quite how the matter developed: Morley and Harcourt were frightened by the Nonconformists. Gladstone surrendered to Morley and Harcourt. We may regret this, but we cannot entirely be surprised at it. Gladstone was himself eighty-one and might die at any moment. Morley was his political son. Harcourt had the succession of Gladstone in the leadership of the Commons. It was difficult to resist the wishes of the younger generation expressed on a problem which affected their future far more than his own. One truth however emerges clearly. Gladstone did not sustain the rôle of a sanctimonious humbug.

Parnell turned on the "unrivalled sophist" with a savagery that it is impossible to commend. But, if the misfortunes of others be of any consolation to the dead, Parnell should be consoled. Gladstone carried, to the end, the Parnellite hook in his mouth. The Home Rule cause did not recover from the shock of the scandal. The 1892 election, when it came, did not fulfil the hopes of 1890, and Gladstone formed his fourth

[1] Ervine, *Life of Parnell*, p. 276.

administration with a majority of about forty. To force a Home Rule Bill through the Commons with such a majority, and at the age of eighty-four, was an amazing achievement, moral, physical, and intellectual. But it was also futile, and it is absurd to blame the House of Lords for throwing the measure out.

The Home Rule Bill defeated, the Government decided to continue with the less controversial measures of the "Newcastle Programme," as the new Liberal platform was called. But the same fate which had overtaken the Home Rule Bill lay in wait for the minor measures, and Mr. Gladstone, with a sound instinct and indomitable nerve, suggested an appeal to the country on the whole attitude of the House of Lords towards the Liberal programme. The brain reels before the spectacle of a man of eighty-four seriously proposing to take the lead in a political campaign of such magnitude. His younger colleagues were, however, more prudent and opposed the suggestion. Hence his last speech, which did not reveal all his desires, was delivered in the House of Commons on March 1st, 1894, on the loss of the Parish Councils Bill, and laid down the lines along which the Liberal Party was to develop :

"We are compelled to accompany that acceptance with the sorrowful declaration that the differences, not of a temporary or casual nature merely, but differences of conviction, differences of prepossession, differences of mental habit, and differences of fundamental tendency, between the House of Lords and the House of Commons appear to have reached a development in the present years such as to create a state of things of which we are compelled to say that, in our judgment, it cannot continue. . . . The issue which is raised between a deliberative assembly elected by the vote of more than 6,000,000 people and a deliberative assembly occupied by many men of virtue, by many men of talent, of course with considerable diversities and varieties, is a controversy which, when once raised, must go forward to an issue."

"Men did not know," writes Morley, "that they were listening to his last speech, but his words fell in with the eager humour of his followers round him and he sat down amid vehement plaudits. Then when the business was at an end he rose and for the last time walked away from the House of Commons. He had first addressed it sixty-one years before."

. . . .

No, men did not know that this was the great leader's last speech ; still less did they guess the reasons why it should be. Evidently Gladstone had got to go some time or other. The Home Rule Bill was defeated. Gladstone was suffering from increasing cataract and deafness. He was eighty-four. So he had gone. The hideous truth, hidden both from Court and Parliament, was a very different matter. Gladstone had resigned upon the Navy Estimates. The battle he had won against Palmerston in the 'sixties, he lost against his own colleagues thirty years later. Lord Spencer's Naval Estimates were judged by Gladstone to be grossly excessive. On the other hand, three admirals threatened to resign if they were not accepted, and Gladstone had no supporter among his own colleagues save Morley and Shaw Lefevre. The question was held up in the hopes of accommodation ; and no accommodation came. At the same time the Cabinet also refused, against the advice of Gladstone, to appeal to the country on the Parish Councils Bill. Gladstone must go. His colleagues did not want him. What a nuisance he was ! When he said he was a Liberal he really meant it. He thought that economy in armaments really had some meaning : that Home Rule was a principle worth fighting for. This was intolerable. And lucky was it for Gladstone that he should have resigned upon the Estimates, " the worst ever submitted to Parliament," he remarked. " This led him to recur to the beginning of it this time last year (trouble in the Cabinet over Navy Estimates), and he spoke rather scornfully of the surrender of the Government to the threat of three admirals to resign. He dwelt on the hopelessness of arriving at any principle of limitation in regard to naval expenditure, which he likened to the rents men paid for deer forests, purely fanciful and boundlessly extravagant."[1] And again, "Mr. Gladstone reverted to the £22,000,000 Naval Estimates, urging that such an expenditure was an invitation to the powers to combine and a justification of their recent attitude towards England. He denies that it is a called-for answer to a plain challenge. He regards it rather as a challenge on our side."

[1] Rendel, *Personal Papers*, p. 107.

The affectionate Morley looked on in anguish at the collapse of the G.O.M.'s policy, and the departure of the G.O.M. It also fell to him to break the news to Mrs. Gladstone.

" After dinner in the drawing-room, he at once sat down to backgammon with Armistead. Mrs. G. carried me to a sofa behind an ornamental glass screen ; and I then found with a minute of consternation that I was to tell her the fatal news. Mr. G. had said to her on his return from the House that I was coming to dine : that he was fagged, and that I would tell her how things stood. It was as painful as any talk could be. However I had no choice. I told her that the reign was over and that the only question was whether the abdication should be now or in February. The poor lady was not in the least prepared for the actual stroke. Had gone through so many crises and they had all come out right in the end : had calculated that the refreshment of the coming journey to Biarritz would change his thought and purpose. I told her that language had been used which made change almost impossible. Well, then, would not the Cabinet change, when they knew the perils with which his loss would surround them ? I was obliged to keep to iron facts. What a curious scene ! Me breaking to her that the pride and glory of her life was at last to face eclipse, that the curtain was falling on a grand drama of fame, power, acclamation : the rattle of the dice on the backgammon board and the laughter and chucklings of the two long-lived players sounded a strange running refrain."

There followed the last painful interview with the Queen.

" Then came the conversation," notes Mr. Gladstone, " which may be called neither here nor there. Its only material feature was negative. There was not one syllable of the past except a repetition, an emphatic repetition, of the thanks she had long ago amply rendered for what I had done, a service of no great merit, in the case of the Duke of Coburg, and which I assured her would not now escape my notice if occasion should arise. There was the question of eyes and ears, of German versus English oculists, she believing in the German as decidedly superior. Some reference to my wife, with whom she had an interview, and had ended it affectionately – and various nothings. . . . Was I wrong in not tendering orally my best wishes ? I was afraid that anything said by me should have the appearance of *touting*."

A letter was also tended to the Queen in a box and to this she replied :

"Though the Queen has already accepted Mr. Gladstone's resignation and has taken leave of him she does not like to leave his letter tendering his resignation unanswered. She therefore writes these few lines to say that she thinks that after so many years of arduous labour and responsibility, he is right in wishing to be relieved at his age of these arduous duties. And she trusts he will be able to enjoy peace and quiet with his excellent and devoted wife in health and happiness and that his eyesight may improve. The Queen would gladly have conferred a peerage on Mr. Gladstone, but she knows he would not accept it."

Thus the Queen took leave of that one of her Prime Ministers, who had most respect for the throne.

Gladstone mused long and sadly over his relations with his Sovereign, and writes in his diary for January 2nd, 1896 :

"While it is on my mind, I place on record here, awaiting some more formal method, my strong desire that after my decease my family shall be most careful to keep in the background all information respecting the personal relations of the Queen and myself during these later years down to 1894, when they died a kind of natural death."

In February '97 he again noted :

"I do not speak lightly when I state my convictions that the circumstances of my farewell, which I think were altogether without parallel, had serious causes beyond the operation of political disagreements, which no doubt went for something but which were insufficient to explain them. Statements, whether true or false, must have been carried to her ears, which in her view required (and not merely allowed) the mode of proceeding which was actually adopted."

This veiled statement hints, it has been thought, that the Queen had heard and believed the absurd tittle-tattle of the clubs about Gladstone's supposed relations with women of the town, tittle-tattle which was rife in London through the 'nineties, and which was only silenced by the Wright *v.* Gladstone case of 1927.

The Queen, exercising privilege, did not seek Gladstone's advice as to his successor. He would have advised Lord Spencer, but she sent for Lord Rosebery, whom Gladstone, much to his subsequent regret, had appointed Foreign Secretary in an endeavour to be agreeable to Court. A general sense of relief was experienced. Any number of ships could now be built ; and, on his very first day as Prime Minister, Rosebery stated that England was the predominant partner, whose conversion to Home Rule was a prerequisite to its concession : true enough, no doubt, but coming at such a moment, it could have but one meaning. The Liberal Party intended to throw over Home Rule, as it had already adopted imperialism ; and so the Party marched blithely onwards under the guidance of the Liberal League, till it ended abjectly and for ever in the swamps of the world war.

Gladstone lived for four years more, to see everything he stood for getting more and more discredited. The cancer of imperialism ate deeper into the bones of the British State, till the Old Man became sorry that he had lived to see the day. " I am contented with my half century," he said more than once, " I do not envy my successors." The great democratic leader was never more remote from his following than in the final years of his apotheosis. His physique had always been marvellous, though he had a tendency to influenza and high temperature. But in 1897, he became subject to severe pain behind his cheek and nose, and cancer of the eye was diagnosed.[1] The man who had known so little pain, who had functioned so perfectly, was to spend a year of almost ceaseless agony.

> " He is terribly depressed," writes Lord Rendel in January, 1898, " and for most of the twenty-four hours he is under pain, which at its lowest point is discomfort, but at its height most intense suffering. . . . Mr. G.'s depression is mainly due as he admits to the unnerving and unmanning effect of protracted suffering. He says he is a ' broken man.' But he is actively sensible of the loss of his power of in any way profitably spending his time. For this reason alone he would wish it were God's will that the end should

[1] This terrible illness is thought to have originated in his being struck in the eye by a piece of gingerbread, in Chester on June 25th, 1892.

be at once. And another great trial to him is his keen sense of the trouble he thinks he gives. He cannot bear to discompose us by giving evidence of pain. He regards himself as a heavy and useless burden. Last night after a short paroxysm of pain in the drawing room, which of course caused silence and some consternation, he said three times to himself, 'I cumber the ground.' But he maintains that God has some good purpose and he submits himself. 'It is God's will.'"

The pain continuing, it was thought advisable to try the air of Bournemouth, whither he was taken on February 22nd, 1898, and on March 18th he learned, with a sense of unutterable relief, that he was only likely to live a few weeks. On the 22nd he returned to Hawarden to die. Music was his chief consolation "the old composers being those he liked best to hear." His private secretary and admirer, Arthur Godley, gives a gentler account of him right at the end.

"My next visit was in May, 1898, when I was summoned from Hawarden to London to see him for the last time, a few days before his death. He was then in a perfectly peaceful state apparently suffering no pain, sitting up in a large armchair and talking to me almost as he might have talked before his illness, asking me about my various belongings and especially about Hugh at Oxford. I was in his room for perhaps rather more than five minutes and my impression of him is one that it is altogether pleasant to recall: the great stillness, the bright sunshine pouring in at the open window, the feeling that the worst was over and that rest was at hand. He died on Ascension Day, May the 19th, and in the evening I went to Church and heard quite unexpectedly in the lesson for the day the repeated question 'Knowest thou the Lord will take thy master from thy head to-day?' and the answer 'Yea, I know it.'"[1]

[1] Lord Kilbracken, *Reminiscences*, pp. 220–1.

It is easy to pick holes in Gladstone's mind. He is said to lack genius and in a way he did. He was uncritical in many things, and, as he said himself, he " lacked the higher imagination of the artist." Despite his breadth of mind and width of interest, which extended from Saint Augustine to Marie Bashkirtzeff, his table-talk often leaves a quality of commonplaceness about it. His religious beliefs were unnecessarily literal. His Homeric studies were childish and grotesque. He was too fond of turning to books, rather than to thought. This quality amazed his contemporaries, but it was in fact a weakness. " We began talking on political and theological subjects," writes Dr. Döllinger, " and became both of us so engrossed with the conversation that it was two o'clock at night when I left the room to fetch a book from my library, bearing on the matter in hand. I returned with it in a few minutes and found him deep in a volume he had drawn out of his pocket – true to his principle of never wasting time – during my momentary absence." Yet the " wasted " moments are often the most valuable in life, and we turn with a sense of relief to a sentence in a letter of Disraeli's where he observes that he never minds having to waste an hour at a railway station " as one can always think." Gladstone would have been only too prone to pull some second-rate book out of his pocket and flatter himself that he was spending the time profitably.

Compared with Disraeli, he lacked originality. "I have been a learner all my life," he said; and if he is a genius, he is a genius as Raphael was a genius, a man of immense digestive faculty, with the power of slowly and healthily absorbing whatever came in his way. All his life he had undergone "influences," first that of Canning, then that of Peel, of Bright in the crucial 'sixties, and finally, and very powerfully, of Acton.

The strange paradox is that this learner should have been so excitable, so almost uncontrolled in his passion, and that this passion should have gone with such a love of sophistical argument and so much earnestness, an earnestness which had a ridiculous side, and led him into speaking on occasion in rather an absurd manner. A distinguished Liberal "asked Mr. Gladstone if he did not think it a matter of regret that the young men of the time seemed to take so little interest in the debates in the House of Commons. Mr. Gladstone laid his hand on my friend's arm and explained with awe-inspiring emphasis that the indifference thus shown by the rising generation appeared to him to be 'a plague-spot' on the body politic."[1] Similarly, those who have enjoyed the friendship of Gladstone have described to me the tense expression and flashing eye with which he would play beggar-my-neighbour. Once, when going over Chequers, he came upon a parrot who spoke modern Greek. Gladstone,

[1] Tollemache, *Talks with Mr. Gladstone*, p. 30.

all enthusiasm, responded with a long quotation from Homer and could not hide his disappointment, when the bird failed to reply. Similarly, Gladstone explaining the beauties of his rather chipped collection of old china, or passionately enquiring the price of everything in a shop, his invariable custom when abroad, appeared to the common man slightly ridiculous.

We will admit that this shows a considerable absence of proportion and of the form of self-consciousness called humour. But it was his strength as well as his weakness. It was his intense vitality that enabled this most solitary man to force himself upon the community and compel it to accept him as its leader. "He is not a brain," somebody once said, "but a body."

By his vitality he enhanced the value of the subjects which he was treating. While he was alive no one was allowed to think that the good government of the city was a matter of secondary importance. Gladstone lived through the golden age of the Parliamentary system, and was the master technician, whom the requirements of that system had called into being.

It is on this point that Mr. Balfour seized, in his speech on Gladstone's death :

"One service he did in my opinion quite incalculable, which is altogether apart from the judgment that we may be supposed to pass on particular opinions or particular lines of policy which Mr. Gladstone may, from time to time, have advocated. Sir, he added a dignity, a weight to the deliberations of this house by his genius, which I think it is impossible adequately to replace. It is not enough for us to keep up simply a level though it be a high level, of probity and patriotism. The mere average of civic virtue is not sufficient to preserve this assembly from the fate that has overcome so many other assemblies, products of democratic forces. More than this is required : more than this was given by Mr. Gladstone. He brought to our debates a genius which compelled attention, he raised in the public estimation the whole level of our proceedings, and they will be most ready to admit the infinite value of his service who realise how much of public prosperity is involved in the maintenance of the worth of public life, and how perilously difficult most democracies apparently find it to avoid the opposite dangers into which so many of them have fallen."

It seems unnecessary to adorn the tale. Whatever may have been his failings as a statesman and his limitations as an intellect, there was never anything mediocre in his nature. Though unsuccessful in many of the battles he waged most fiercely, he could on occasion raise the democracy to his own level. Anxious no doubt to gain power, he never feared to lose it, if honour required ; and since his day, few enough have been the statesmen who have ever even tried to direct the forces of public opinion.

SELECTED BIBLIOGRAPHY

Morley : *Life of Gladstone.*

Morley : *Reminiscences.*

A. T. Bassett : *Selected Speeches of Gladstone.*

Gladstone, W. E. : *Speeches in Scotland* (Vols. I., II.) (Midlothian Campaign).

Philip Guedalla : *Palmerston and Gladstone.*

Hirst : *Gladstone as Economist and Financier.*

Lord Gladstone : *After Thirty Years.*

Lord Kilbracken : *Reminiscences.* The best intimate sketch.

Lord Rendel : *Personal Papers.* Specially for the last three years.

Queen Victoria : *Correspondence.* Specially 1879–1886.

L. J. Jennings : *Mr. Gladstone.* A brilliant hostile sketch.

Barry O'Brien : *Life of Parnell.*

St. John Ervine : *Life of Parnell.*

Bernard Allen : *Gordon and the Sudan.*

Lytton Strachey : *Eminent Victorians. Queen Victoria.*

G. E. Buckle : *Life of Lord Beaconsfield.* Specially Vols. V., VI.

D. C. Somervell : *Gladstone and Disraeli.*

Among others, to whom I owe much, I would particularly thank Mr. J. L. Hammond for his sympathy and advice, and his endless willingness to put his superior knowledge at my disposal ; and my erudite young friend Mr. Richard White, whose forthcoming work on Mr. Gladstone and the American Civil War will be appreciated by all Gladstone students.

student council grant
paging O.K.